Nov '75

Happy Birthday

Jenny   + Bill
  x x x x

How the Lions Won

How the Lions Won

*The stories and skills behind
two famous victories*

EDITED BY
TERRY O'CONNOR

COLLINS
St James's Place, London
1975

William Collins Sons & Co Ltd
London · Glasgow · Sydney · Auckland
Toronto · Johannesburg

This book is dedicated to
the wives of the Lions and the wives
of all those who have followed the
Lions on tour

First published 1975
© Terry O'Connor 1975
ISBN 0 00 211364 3
Set in Monotype Baskerville
Made and printed in Great Britain by
William Collins Sons & Co Ltd Glasgow

Contents

Foreword by J. A. Tallent   9
Editor's Note   13

Part One: The Lions in Perspective

TERRY O'CONNOR
Where We Went Wrong   19
Turning Right   36
Believing in Victory   45
Pride of the Lions   58

Part Two: Eight Lions

SYD MILLAR
The Challenge to Rugby   75
Coaching – Key to Team Work   86

WILLIE JOHN MCBRIDE
I Would Like to Live it all Again   95
Line-out Play   118

IAN MCLAUCHLAN
From Mickey to Mighty   122
Scrummaging   127

FRAN COTTON
Kitted Out for Wigan   140
Rucking and Mauling   145

FERGUS SLATTERY
Triple Crown Baby   153
The Pivot Five   163

GARETH EDWARDS
The Old Enemy, England   178
The Scrum-Half   190

CONTENTS

MIKE GIBSON

Pressure Produces Players   197
The Three-quarter's Skills   200

J. P. R. WILLIAMS

It's Frightening Watching Myself on Television   207
Back Line Attacks   212

Part Three: The Opposition Speaks

COLIN MEADS

The Lions in New Zealand   227

HANNES MARAIS

The South African Tour   233

Appendices: The Lions' Record

1. Lions Tour of New Zealand 1971   241
2. Lions Tour of South Africa 1974   248

List of Illustrations
and Acknowledgments

1	Syd Miller	*opposite page* 80
2 and 3	The Lions Captain in South Africa – Willie John McBride	81
4 and 5	The strategists who beat New Zealand – John Dawes and Barry John	96
6 and 7	Tries in dispute: South Africa, the fourth and final Test	97
8 and 9	Quality Possession – in New Zealand and South Africa	192
10 and 11	Defence and Attack	193
12 and 13	Stars in New Zealand – David Duckham and Gerald Davies	208
14 and 15	. . . and in South Africa – J. P. R. Williams, Andy Irvine and Mike Gibson	209

DIAGRAMS

Scrum Channels	139
Back Row Ploys	220
The Miss	221
Dummy Crash	222
Miss J. P. R.	223

ACKNOWLEDGMENTS

John Rubython – 1; Colorsport – 2, 4, 5, 9, 11, 14, 15, 16; Peter Bush – 3, 10, 13; G. Hofmeister – 6; die Burgher – 7;

ACKNOWLEDGMENTS

Evening News, Wellington – 8; *Dominion*, Wellington – 12. All Colorsport photographs by Colin Elsey. I would also like to thank Michael Nimmo, who helped both in the editing and compiling the statistics, and Colin Elsey who was a constant source of advice over the photographs. Finally, my thanks to Harrold King for putting up with a stream of corrections from myself and Syd Miller during the planning of the diagrams.

Foreword

J. A. TALLENT

*Chairman of the Four Home Unions. Former England
player 1931–35. President of the Rugby Union 1959–60*

Why, after nearly fifty years of failure to win a series – the
first full British Lions team toured South Africa in 1924 – has
success been achieved in two successive tours? The answer
lies in improved coaching and administration. I will take the
latter first as it came before the explosion in coaching in the
British Isles.

As far back as 1966, the Four Home Rugby Union Tours
Committee were unhappy with the results of that year's
British Lions tour to Australia and New Zealand. A major
tour takes three years to set up, and as we were due in South
Africa in 1968 time was vital. In November 1966 the committee made certain important decisions. First, the manager
and assistant manager would be chosen one year before a
tour. Next, the committee defined clearly the respective
duties of the management and directed that in future the
officers of the committee would brief the Lions management
after the appointment of the captain and before the team's
departure. In March 1967 a further decision was made, that
the manager would be chairman of the selection committee,
with a casting vote only, one selector coming from each of the
Four Home Unions, as previously.

That same month, March 1967, John Hart (Scotland) and
I were appointed secretary and chairman respectively of the
Tours Committee, and our first task was to organise the
meeting at which David Brooks (England) and Ronnie
Dawson (Ireland) were appointed manager and assistant
manager for the British Isles tour to South Africa in 1968.

9

This policy has undoubtedly given the management the opportunity of watching and getting to know likely players during the season before their selection, usually in March.

Before the 1974 tour the committee decided that the assistant manager was also to be co-opted to the selection committee – a result of the strong recommendation of Dr Doug Smith (Scotland) and Carwyn James (Wales) in their report on the 1971 tour. These reports, incidentally, provide an up-to-date link between committee and management, whilst the briefing sessions have ensured that the management know their individual tasks and how they relate to one another.

The Tours Committee over this period were blessed with two first-class secretaries in John Hart and now Albert Agar (England). With the improvement in communications, management and the officers of the Tours Committee can keep in close contact and a replacement can be in South Africa in three days, in New Zealand in four.

Against this background coaching as we know it today was born. After certain problems not unusual with a delayed birth the child flourished and was undoubtedly the greatest single factor in the success of the recent tours. In 1968 I watched Ronnie Dawson hold the initial training periods at Eastbourne, and it is a fact that he had to start by teaching most of his players the basic skills. Despite this, the team had a better record than it was ever given credit for.

In 1971 Carwyn James, again at Eastbourne, was bubbling over with ideas, but this time his players were able to accept them. He was perhaps the most imaginative coach yet and had splendid support from his captain, John Dawes.

Finally, in 1974, I saw Syd Millar take his first training session at Roehampton. Any doubts that, because he had only recently stopped playing himself, he might be too close to the team were immediately dispelled and, as you will read in this book, his views on the game and knowledge of coaching are all-embracing. With Alun Thomas (Wales) dealing competently with the manifold extraneous problems of a tour,

Syd was able to concentrate with his great captain, Willie John McBride, on the task of beating the Springboks.

The explosion in coaching in the British Isles really occurred between 1968 and 1971. The appointment of Ray Williams (Wales) and Don Rutherford (England) as technical advisers to their respective Unions and of the subsequent national coaches has had a profound effect on the material available today to the Lions selectors. It has also improved the standard of applicants for the post of assistant manager: three national coaches were in the running for the last tour.

The Home Unions may have been slow to adopt coaches in the style used by New Zealand and South Africa for many years, but, once we did, two factors helped to give us the advantage. First, the ideas of the coaches of the Four Home Unions, each with their own emphasis, are wonderful material on which a Lions coach can draw and mould his players. Second, the overseas Unions, having experienced success for so long with the same methods, were unprepared for something both basic and sophisticated.

To analyse the difference between the two victorious teams is not easy. In 1971 we sent away the best set of backs since the 1955 side to South Africa. The forwards were more suspect but rose to the occasion superbly. The 1974 side had, to my mind, the best sixteen forwards ever to represent a British Isles touring team, with the key positions of scrum-half and full-back doubly covered. The strength of the forwards and the fact that the backs came good was undoubtedly due to coaching and the superb team spirit generated by their captain. I shall never forget their great performance in the second international in Pretoria.

The genius and ability of some of the great players of the '20s and '30s compare favourably with any of today's, but undoubtedly the player of potential now stands a better chance of becoming a British Lion through the coaching he receives on leaving school, and the way he is watched and studied by management and selectors. My one fear is that coaching may be overdone and kill the natural flair of the individual player.

I was delighted when asked to write this foreword by Terry O'Connor, that great enthusiast for our game. It gives me the opportunity of paying tribute not only to those who have contributed to this book, but also to the others, both management and players. They were all dedicated, disciplined and friendly men to whom the world of sport owes much. Their views make fascinating reading and must surely be of value to the future development of rugby football, wherever it is played.

Editor's Note

Returning by air from South Africa at the end of the 1974 Lions tour I was approached by some of the party with an idea which gave birth to this book. The Lions were justly proud of their achievement in becoming the first team to win a major Test series in South Africa this century, as they were of their similar triumph in New Zealand in 1971, and they considered they had a story worth telling, one which could benefit rugby football and improve the standard of play. Throughout South Africa they had frequently been approached by rugby enthusiasts keen to discover the 'secret' of the Lions' success. Couldn't I write about that success in a book? The idea was an appealing one.

However, early thoughts of a short, quickly prepared account were quickly discarded, since the elite band of Lions who had been assembled made it obvious that together they could produce a fascinating and original book of a far more lasting quality than something hurried through by an outside commentator.

Later, after discussions with Willie John McBride and Syd Millar in Northern Ireland, it was decided that just another 'coaching manual' would limit the book's appeal and would fail to give the necessary background to *How the Lions Won*. Rugby after all is a game where the character and attitude of players is as important as the skills and the strategies adopted. The Lions' story would only be half told if, for example, Gareth Edwards were to write solely about the tactical approach to being a scrum-half without giving the background of how he developed into one of the finest players ever to appear on a rugby field, or how his skills actually worked in practice.

That is why each of the main contributors to this book has written both an autobiographical note and a coaching chapter. The emphasis is always on explaining exactly how each person himself came to learn the skills he now puts into practice. The importance of scrummaging, for instance, which is the book's most constant theme, comes across not through some dry exposition but through the way the players concerned with scrummaging came to see what they had to do. This, after all, is how people learn in life.

When my band of players were gathered together I was lucky that, with the exception of the Englishman, Fran Cotton, they had all played on both the 1971 and the 1974 tours. Those who contributed were also chosen so that every aspect of rugby could be covered, from the front row to full back. Naturally their contributions vary in style and length. Players like Mike Gibson and Gareth Edwards may share the same range of skills on the rugby field but in their home environments they are very contrasting individuals. Edwards is a volatile Welshman who speaks about rugby with a bubbling passion, while Gibson is a precise Northern Irishman, whose legal background ensures he wastes few words!

Although both tours are dealt with in detail it was also inevitable that there should be a greater emphasis on the trip to South Africa, because that was the more recent of the two tours and was the culmination of the Lions' successes. Triumphs often develop from failures, and ironically it is fortunate that McBride experienced three tours as the member of a losing side. His story reveals his personal agony of playing with teams that were inefficient and unable to bring the best out of themselves. More than any other man, McBride can illustrate the changing face of the Lions from the low depths of the '60s to the dizzy heights achieved during the '70s.

Syd Millar's comprehensive contribution of coaching acknowledges the work of Carwyn James in 1971 and the many others who helped bring about the new approach. There are those who regret the efficiency which now dominates rugby in Britain and Ireland, but these same people also criticise the defeats in the past. It is obvious from the contributions which follow that the players themselves welcome the changes in attitude and coaching that have made it possible to weld their individual talents into a winning combination.

The best summary of the modern Lions was made by Anton Oberholzer, the Transvaal captain, in a prophetic speech mid-way through the 1974 tour. After his team had been beaten 23–15 at Ellis Park, Johannesburg, he told an audience of some two hundred: 'You have just seen one of the greatest teams in history, and I am convinced they will still be unbeaten at the end of the tour. For the past seventy years Lions teams have visited this country and often played magnificently, but failed to win a Test series. This time they are different. The college boys have been left at home and they have included only men.'

Finally, no game exists without an opposition, and it is only right that Colin Meads, who captained New Zealand in 1971, and Hannes Marais, the skipper of the 1974 Springboks, should have their say. They are complimentary to the Lions but not uncritical, and their contributions are the better for that. Rugby is a continuing story, and since the end of the Lions tour in 1974 it is obvious that New Zealand and South Africa have taken to heart the lessons of defeat. As John Dawes, the Lions captain of 1971, has said, future tours to the Southern Hemisphere will become more difficult, not easier.

May 1975   TERRY O'CONNOR

Part One

THE LIONS
IN PERSPECTIVE

TERRY O'CONNOR

Where We Went Wrong

To understand how the Lions won and changed the balance of power from the Southern to Northern Hemisphere after seventy years of failure it is important to trace the story from the past. During those years New Zealand and South African teams were the masters on their home grounds and in the British Isles. They were organised to win while the British players were enslaved by an outdated code of amateurism which should have been buried in the last century. But the modern Lions were helped by the advent of coaching and a few enlightened officials to prepare themselves to win. Players like McBride were motivated by the failures of the past but convinced the Lions had the qualities needed, if given the chance. They did not seek money or fame – just an opportunity to prove themselves.

Bertie Mee, the Arsenal football manager, paid one of the finest of many tributes to the 1974 Lions at a luncheon in Johannesburg. Talking to five members of the team he said, 'I would like to have eleven of you playing for Arsenal next season.' When I asked him what he meant he added: 'Because they want to win.'

Rugby was developed in England during the middle of the last century and in 1888 it was decided to follow the example of cricket and take the game overseas to Australia and New Zealand. In Australia the team of Englishmen and a few Scots under the captaincy of R. L. Seddon, Broughton Rangers (later to become a Rugby League club) were unbeaten after sixteen matches. They discovered the New Zealanders had advanced more rapidly and two out of nineteen games were lost. Three years later a team composed mainly of Cambridge University men went to South Africa and were unbeaten in nineteen games. It was eighty-three years before another British team toured South Africa without losing a match.

The 'colonials' mastered the game rapidly and were fortunate not to be involved with the controversy about broken time which split English rugby in 1893 and had a disastrous effect on official thinking for years to come. For younger readers the phrase 'broken time' will have little meaning but it was an explosive issue during a period when rugby in Britain was developing at a tremendous pace. Briefly, many of the Northern clubs considered their players should be compensated for loss of earnings on Saturday mornings because they had to travel to matches. Officials of other clubs, mainly influenced by the South, considered such payments would lead to professionalism, as had already happened in association football. The motion to allow payment for loss of time was defeated, but it led to the formation of the Northern Union, which later became the professional game Rugby League.

Rugby Union football was therefore saved as an amateur game and is now played in more than sixty countries, whereas professional Rugby is confined to four countries and in England restricted to three counties. But unfortunately the fears of professionalism influenced the progress of the playing side of the game, and for some seventy years coaching and organised competition were discouraged in most of the home countries.

South Africa and New Zealand were not troubled by such inhibitions, and they considered team organisation essential to gain the best results. This is reflected in their performances. During five major tours the Springboks made to the British Isles between 1906 and 1961 they played twenty internationals and lost one. Only Scotland defeated them, in 1906, and England gained a 3–3 draw during the same tour. During a similar period – between 1903 to 1968 – Lions teams on seven tours suffered a similar fate as the home countries. In the twenty-five Test matches played during these years they won only four, drew five and lost sixteen.

New Zealand teams were able to write a similar story of success in the record book. From 1905 to 1967 they sent six All Blacks teams to the home countries and won seventeen of their twenty-two matches, lost four and drew one. Between 1904 to 1966 the Lions' record in New Zealand was even poorer than in South Africa. Of the twenty Test matches played they managed to win only two and drew two.

It was with this depressing background that the Lions undertook a tour to New Zealand in 1971, and three years later another to South Africa. The transformation was remarkable as history now records. In eight Test matches played on the two tours five were won, two drawn and only one lost. More important, both series ended in triumph for the first time this century.

To discover the reason for the change one must again slip back into history. Early Lions tours were given little recognition. It was not until 1950 that a newspaper correspondent – D. R. Gent of the *Sunday Times* – travelled with the team, and he had to return early due to illness. Therefore reports of matches were scanty and there was no public post-tour inquest on the reason for repeated failures. Also, before the second world war it was more difficult for the Lions to send their best players because of difficulties over work and money. Ray Longland (Northampton), an outstanding English prop, would have been a certain selection for the 1938 team to South Africa but he could not raise the £50 necessary to guarantee he would not be a financial embarrassment. This money was needed to ensure that players had sufficient pocket money, because it was recognised that the allowance (three shillings a day) was not sufficient. The 1971 and 1974 Lions received only 75p per day but attracted gates in excess of £3,000,000.

Selection of those men available was not sound, either, because those given the job of nominating the players had little or no experience of the conditions on tour. Some players become better under stress, while others wilt. Such considerations were seldom taken into account. Nomination

of tour officials was little better. Availability was often the
main criterion for the appointment of a manager. In 1950 the
determining factor in the selection of an assistant manager
was his ability to write shorthand. More important, until
1968 the officials were appointed so late that they could play
no part in finding the team they had to manage on tour.

The first Lions tour to make any major impact on the sporting public was 1955, when the series against the Springboks
was drawn 2–2. Three British newspapermen covered that
tour and therefore it was the first to be widely reported. Such
was the talent in the team they managed to beat South Africa
twice without the advantages of a coach or sound team planning before the tour. Fortunately the 1955 Lions had runners
like Cliff Morgan, Tony O'Reilly, Jeff Butterfield and
W. P. C. Davies, and forwards such as Courtney Meredith,
Bryn Meredith, W. O. Williams, Rhys Williams and Jimmy
Greenwood. That team would certainly have won the series if
blessed with the 1971–74 know-how.

By the time the Lions returned to South Africa in 1962 the
national newspaper corps had increased to eight reporters,
an indication of the growing national interest in these tours.
Much credit for the extra coverage should be given to the
foresight of the late J. L. Manning, who at the time was the
sports editor of the *Daily Mail*. More than a year before the
tour was due to take place he decided that I, as the newspaper's rugby correspondent, should go with the Lions. As
is often the case with Fleet Street newspapers, this started a
chain reaction and for the first time *The Times, Daily Express,
Daily Herald, Daily Telegraph* and *Sunday Express* sent cor-
respondents, in addition to the *Sunday Times* and *Western
Mail* (Cardiff).

With so many newspapers' columns devoted to the Lions'
playing activities, the rugby public in Britain and Ireland
were at last made aware of the differences in approach of
their players and the Springboks. More important, the
public were able to understand the tactical aspects of the
game which for too long had been a mystery known only to

the players. This publicity also gave ammunition to the few but growing number of those who advocated coaching.

Brian Vaughan, the former England forward who was manager of the 1962 Lions, did not have the benefits of a coach and took on the job himself. He was one of the best of many managers with whom I have toured. Although some of his players were not of Lions standard he had a number of high quality and developed a pack of forwards worthy of taking on the Springboks. Vaughan was aware it was forward strength which the South Africans respected, and that the scrum was the basis of building a winning team. In this respect he was ahead of his time, but has never received the recognition he deserved.

The 1962 Lions drew the first Test and should have won the second, but they suffered the fate of many teams overseas who find themselves against a sixteenth man – the referee. In this case the Lions pushed the Springboks over their line and wheeled in copybook fashion for Keith Rowlands to touch down, but the referee disallowed the try on the grounds that he had lost sight of the ball. Many Springboks accepted it was a try but the record book shows only that the Lions lost by a penalty goal to nil.

It was two years later, also in South Africa, that another significant tour took place which was to have a major impact on the thinking of rugby in the home countries. Wales, a country with a passion and national fervour for rugby equalled only in New Zealand and South Africa, undertook their first-ever tour overseas. Wales met South Africa in the sunshine of Durban but played as if the conditions were the same as the rain and wind so often found in Cardiff. For the first half the Springboks allowed themselves to be dominated by the touch-kicking tactics of the Welsh captain Clive Rowlands and the score was even at 3–3. Once the home team realised that the Welsh could be beaten by running the ball, especially by their forwards, the game changed drama-tically and the final score was 24–3.

This was one of the heaviest defeats Wales had ever

suffered and it was considered a disgrace in the valleys where rugby is a way of life. Unlike Lions' tours, when Wales could put the blame for defeat on players from other countries, this time they realised how far they were behind. Alun Thomas, who was then assistant manager and who was later to manage the Lions in 1974, became a strong advocate of coaching. This was later taken up by the Welsh Rugby Union and they instructed the clubs to find coaches.

There was little resistance because Welshmen never again wanted to suffer the shame of a 24–3 defeat. However, at the famous Cardiff club they stood against the idea on the grounds of tradition, and appointed their captain as coach.

Before 1964 Scotland, Ireland and England had all undertaken short tours and lost their international matches, but were not moved by the same spirit for change like the Welsh. Pleading they were amateurs, they did not consider defeat was a reason for change. However, the need for organised team planning was being talked about, and eventually the Rugby Union of England brought together a number of men who had studied the tactical side of the game and produced an important book – *A Guide for Coaches*.

The pressure of the media coverage of Lions' tours had also influenced the thinking of some administrators, and it was considered a significant breakthrough when the Lough-borough Colleges coach and 1950 Lion John Robins was appointed assistant manager of the 1966 team. But that familiar stumbling block of tradition meant he was not named coach, and I realised one evening following a Loughborough Colleges dinner that the advance had been only slight. One of the guests was that respected former referee Cyril Gadney, a past R.U. president, and member of the powerful Four Home Unions Committee responsible for selection of Lions teams and officials. When I asked him whether Robins's job would be to coach the team in New Zealand he said it was up to the discretion of the captain who would still be in charge of the tactical and playing side of the team. He ignored my plea that a touring team needed a powerful coach.

Robins would have been well suited to the job of coach in view of his success with Loughborough Colleges. This team of students had already made a major impact on the game and many of the tactical moves devised by Robins had been copied by clubs. But change comes slowly in rugby and in 1966 the forces which held dearly to those links with the last century were strong enough to resist professional thinking in an amateur game. To be fair, the moves towards organised team training had just started, and not enough players, even at international level, were ready for the breakthrough which was to come in the '70s.

Ray McLoughlin, the Irish captain, was another who had problems putting across his advanced thinking. His idea of excluding selectors from the dressing room before matches, for instance – so players could concentrate on the game – was not well received. Indeed, some members of the team re-volted even at the idea of getting away from the team hotel and their well-wishers to concentrate on their mental pre-paration for the game. Today McLoughlin would be regarded as an outstanding captain, but at the time he was rejected because he made too much fuss about the importance of winning.

Wales also had a captain of character in Alun Pask. He did not suffer in his own country for wanting to win because fortunately this has always been a motivating force among Welshmen. The mistake Pask made was to be too honest. In a television interview before the 1966 match against Ireland he was asked who he thought would win the game. He replied: 'Well, on form I think it should be Wales.' Oh, the outcry which followed! Pask was considered ungentle-manly for making such a remark. It was expected from a soccer captain, but not in rugby. Some Irishmen also took it to heart, and it was even suggested as the reason why Wales lost 9–6.

All this meant the position of captaincy of the Lions was

still open when the selectors met in Edinburgh in March following the Calcutta Cup match between Scotland and England. No outstanding candidate emerged from that game, and the final choice of Mike Campbell-Lamerton was a shock to everyone, including the player himself. He did not think he would even be selected, and had arranged a holiday in Spain. Campbell-Lamerton had toured with the Lions in 1962 as a lock forward, but to give extra weight to the pack had been used twice in Test matches as No. 8. He was a whole-hearted player, it is true, but his experience of captaincy and tactical knowledge were limited.

Unfortunately Campbell-Lamerton believed, like some of the officials, that the captain should be in charge of the playing side of the tour and he was determined not to relinquish any of his power. He was obsessed with what he called 'man management' and to his own cost, and to that of the team, he took on too much responsibility. The manager was Des O'Brien, a charming Irishman who was prevented by bad selection from touring with the 1950 Lions. He failed to curtail Campbell-Lamerton's passionate desire to run the show. And Robins, who had helped to pioneer coaching in Britain, was unable to make the impact his talents deserved because the Home Unions had not given him the right brief.

On that 1966 trip the Lions still had eight matches in Australia, and even went on to play further games in Canada on the way home. The Australian part of the trip was a legacy of the past when that country was originally considered more important in rugby terms than New Zealand. But Rugby Union is not a major sport in Australia and the best players and clubs are confined to the states of New South Wales and Queensland. In Victoria the game of Australian Rules dominates, while Rugby League is also rated higher than the Union game in New South Wales and Queensland. In a city like Sydney, which produces the majority of leading League and Union players, there is little attraction in remaining an amateur. This is part of the reason why so many top Australian Union players cash in on their ability and play as professionals. They are not required to move or even change jobs to be paid for playing. Under these circumstances it is extremely difficult for the Wallabies to build teams good enough to play Test matches on level terms with the Lions, All Blacks and Springboks. They are also handicapped by some of the worst referees I have seen, and this must inevitably ruin the development of their players.

So the Australian part of the 1966 tour hindered rather than helped the development of the Lions. They had an unbeaten run of eight matches and finished with a 31–0 victory in the second Test which created a false illusion of greatness. When Freddie Allen, the New Zealand coach, heard that result he decided to give up smoking and increase his training runs. 'I thought this must be an exceptional Lions team and I would need to set an example of fitness to my players,' he said.

At times Australia have produced outstanding teams. As their overall sporting success proves, they have the right approach, and they make excellent rugby tourists. During the '60s they enjoyed many triumphs under the leadership of John Thornett, and they managed to retain the services of players like Ken Catchpole who ranks in the top five among scrum-halves over the last twenty years. The speed he moved the ball was an asset to his team and helped the 1966–67 Wallabies in the British Isles to develop into an excellent attacking side and gain victories over Wales and England. Even Gareth Edwards, Chris Laidlaw, Sid Going or Dawie de Villiers did not move the ball with the speed of Catchpole. He never needed to wind up to make a pass. But unfortunately for the 1966 Lions the Australians were unable to provide the right initiation needed for the rugged approach they were to find in New Zealand.

Rugby in New Zealand, like Wales, is a way of life. Young New Zealanders are weaned on the exploits of the All Blacks, and it is natural they should nurse ambitions to wear the black strip with the silver fern. As New Zealand is primarily a rural community it is only natural their rugby should have an earthy quality. When I first saw the game played in New Zealand on that 1966 tour I was amazed at the fierce physical approach.

One had become familiar with New Zealand rucking during their tours to Britain, but what an experience it was to see it in the province of Otago, where it originally developed under the coaching of the Kavanagh family. The Otago forwards hunted as an eight-man pack and it was literally true that a blanket would have covered all of them for most of the game. They were prepared to go in a foot off the ground without showing any regard to the boots of their own players which often caused injuries. Rucking, and now the maul, are two of the most important developments in rugby football and have given a new dimension to forward play. In the days when forwards were regarded as ball-winners for the backs and needed only to be fit enough to move from scrums to line-outs the second phase did not exist. This all changed with the New Zealand development of rucking.

Vic Kavanagh, a former Otago coach, explained how it came about: 'In my early days with the province we did not have backs with the ability to score against a sound defence. Therefore it was decided the best way to create a three-to-two situation was to take one of the opposing backs out of the defence. Otago forwards have always been good at winning set-ball and this was used to create the second phase by taking an attack over the advantage line and setting up a ruck. Often one of the opposition backs would become tied up and it was therefore easier for our own to score. One of Otago's finest tries came when the forwards won four consecutive rucks and the backs were able to cross the line virtually unopposed.'

This was a type of rugby which few British players really understood when the Lions arrived in New Zealand in 1966. The first match, against Southland, the province at the tip of the South Island, proved a shattering ordeal. Not only did the Lions experience the change from the sunshine of Australia to the cold climate of the deep south, but they came up against an aggressive approach they were not equipped to combat. They were well beaten and went on to lose their first three Saturday games. These defeats exposed the frailty of the team's management which had not been noticed during the triumphant trip round Australia. Campbell-Lamerton, who had taken complete control of the tactical side of the game, sought the advice of New Zealand coaches and consequently became more confused. So did the team.

At the same time it would be wrong to heap the blame entirely on Campbell-Lamerton's shoulders. The fault could be better traced to the thinking in British rugby at the time. In many clubs the captain was the sole selector and in complete charge of the tactical side of the game. I find it difficult to understand how such a ridiculous system had come about, and can only imagine it was another safety valve to avoid any movement towards professionalism. It was the type of thinking which arrested development.

There have been some outstanding club captains, like John Dawes with London Welsh, who of course went on to lead the successful 1971 Lions team to New Zealand, but they are exceptions. Most men who captain club sides lack the knowledge or experience to act also as coach. Dawes was a natural leader and after he retired became the Welsh international coach. Campbell-Lamerton did not have these qualities, but as a soldier believed it was his duty to carry out the instruction of the Four Home Unions who had given him the authority. Robins was confined to getting the players fit, which was an insult to a man with a superb background at Loughborough Colleges plus experience of playing with the Lions in New Zealand in 1950.

Unfortunately Robins tore his achilles tendon during the tour and therefore was unable, even if he had been invited, to play an important part in developing the team during the build-up to the first Test. When the team made the mistake of going to Queenstown – a winter holiday resort – to train for the first Test, Robins was hobbling about on crutches and crying within himself at the lack of urgency about the practice sessions. It was at this period that I first joined the tour, and the training was so haphazard and slapdash that I quickly realised I had come to report a tale of woe rather than success. As the reader will discover throughout this book, winning teams are born from concentration, determination and confidence. None of these qualities existed in the 1966 team.

During the '60s the All Blacks enjoyed one of the golden periods of their rugby history and in boxing terms it was an unfair contest for the 1966 Lions to take them on. In that first Test, at the Carisbrook ground, Dunedin, the New Zealanders were at their peak. Ken Gray, the finest all-round prop I have seen, was able to dominate the front of the line-out, while Colin Meads and his brother Stan locked the pack. They had a formidable trio of loose forwards in Kel Tremain, Brian Lochore and Waka Nathan, and together all eight forwards swept like a black wave over the Lions defence. Only New Zealand's conservative approach to rugby and lack of attacking flair among the backs kept the score down to 20–3.

At the same time the Lions had not done themselves justice. Poor selection and lack of tactical appreciation of the situation prevented their developing as they should. After that first Test Campbell-Lamerton suffered a leg injury which was to handicap him throughout the rest of the tour. Robins, who at one time had seriously considered flying home because he was not allowed to give expression to his ability, had more to do with helping the team prepare for the second Test, which Campbell-Lamerton missed due to injury. For the first time since they left England the two best lock forwards, Willie John McBride and Delme Thomas, were brought together and proved an outstanding success. In later years these two men were to lock many Lions' packs and it is a serious reflection of the 1966 selection that they were kept apart for so long.

There were other fine players among the Lions. Howard Norris, the cheerful Welshman, was a prop of character and skill. Ray McLoughlin was a scrummager of world renown, while Frank Laidlaw was the equal of any hooker in New Zealand. Among the loose forwards Ulsterman Ronnie Lamont played many games during the end of the tour with a damaged shoulder which cut short his career. Jim Telfer, the Scottish No. 8, had the uncompromising attitude of his fellow countrymen. Alun Pask had the ball-handling skill rarely found those days among forwards, while Noel Murphy introduced all the uninhibited enthusiasm of Munster into his play. It was tragic that this sort of spirit was not harnessed to a better team effort.

It is true the backs did not have the skills of the 1959 team which had often run riot during their tour of New Zealand, but Mike Gibson, Dewi Bebb, Dai Watkins, Stuart Wilson and Roger Young had the talents to make up a first-class division if given enough of the ball. Until this tour Gibson had made his name as a fly-half, but he joined the Lions late because of his law exams at Cambridge University and found Watkins – later to win fame in Rugby League as a centre – already established as the No. 1 fly-half. Gibson's versatility and ability enabled him to become the Lions' premier centre.

New Zealanders are good judges of rugby footballers and many I respect regard Gibson as the finest back to visit their islands since the war. During his two tours of 1966 and 1971 he played in all eight Tests as a centre, and only occasionally at fly-half, the position where he won his early fame. Gibson is a 110% player and not satisfied doing just his own job. To use a soccer expression, his 'work rate' is fantastic, especially in defence where his covering has destroyed many promising opposition attacks. Earle Kirton, the former All Black fly-half, uses a colourful expression when comparing Gibson with Barry John, who was hailed as the King of the 1971 team. 'John would not get within a bull's roar of Gibson.' Kirton's critical assessment of John is due to the Welshman's lack of

31

tackling ability, but it does show a lack of appreciation of John's uncanny generalship and brilliant line-kicking.

Wilson was an excellent full-back, and his ability to time his entry into the Lions' three-quarter line produced a number of tries. There was a classic in the final Test scored by right-wing Sandy Hinshelwood. The ball had been won from the end of the line-out and the speed of the movement prevented the All Black loose forwards covering in defence. This attack reflected Robins's influence on the team, and the full-back into the line has become a feature of attacking back play.

Dai Watkins was in the mould of many Welsh fly-halves – small and quick off the mark. He was tried in the centre against Auckland to give Gibson a chance to play in his normal position, but this lasted only ten minutes. Watkins did not then have the defensive ability to play in the centre: he had added two stone in weight without losing his speed when becoming a Rugby League centre of world class. The New Zealanders' ability to read a game enabled the Hawkes Bay coach to discover a weakness in Watkins's game after watching him once, though also on television films of the five-country championship. 'If Watkins breaks left, don't worry,' the coach said, 'he is certain to kick.' This type of tactical appreciation of opposing players' ability is common in Britain today but in 1966 it was rare.

On the left wing the 1966 Lions had Dewi Bebb, who possessed the speed and football guile which would have made him a serious challenger even in the later more successful Lions' sides. Unfortunately in 1966 he seldom received the quality of ball to reveal his true ability.

In the second Test at Wellington the Lions showed such a marked improvement that they lost only 16–12, and might have won if Wilson had been more accurate in his kicking or if the referee, Pat Murphy, had not strangely blown the whistle for a 'forward pass' just before Mike Gibson crossed the All Blacks' line. Wilson was an orthodox rugby kicker and did not register the same high percentage of goals as men like

Barry John, Alan Old and Phil Bennett, who used the soccer kicking style. This is not a conclusive argument for one technique, as Bob Hiller, who toured with the Lions in 1968 and 1971, was a toe-kicker and scored more than a hundred points on both tours without playing in a Test match. Indeed, Hiller had a better average than John in New Zealand. However, there is a lot of evidence that the soccer kick is more accurate at short range, and it is obviously easier to master.

In that second Test the Lions won much more of the ball from the line-out, due to the jumping skill of Thomas. The All Blacks' counter to this was to knock Thomas out of the line as he went for the ball. During that game I remember Thomas being knocked to the ground six times without the ball, and afterwards I asked Pat Murphy why he had not penalised these infringements. He correctly pointed out that he did give one penalty, from which Wilson scored a goal, but claimed he did not see the other incidents. The line-out has always been a highly physical contest to New Zealanders and this had become accepted by their referees. There is no point arguing about the law during the game, and the only real answer is retaliation, as the 1971 Lions team proved. Administrators deplore this approach, but they do not play in Test matches.

New Zealanders have little respect for opponents they can push around. John Graham, flanker in the Wilson Whineray All Blacks who toured the British Isles in 1963–64, was amazed how much scope he was given in the first tour international against England. 'I was opposed to Budge Rogers and he did not counter my tactics, which were designed to prevent him breaking through on our half-backs,' said Graham. 'In New Zealand you always test an opponent in a line-out to see how much you can get away with. I was surprised by the gentlemanly approach of Rogers, who was an excellent player but not aggressive. After this game I thought the international series was going to be easy, assuming that all the flank forwards I met would be like Rogers. I was in for a shock when we played Scotland, because Ronnie Glasgow, whom I marked, retaliated violently immediately I put a hand near him. I was forced to respect Glasgow and this led to a trouble-free game.'

After the good second Test display the spirits of the 1966 Lions were high, and there was hope that with further improvement the series might even be drawn. Unless a team believe in themselves there is little chance of winning. I believe in the principle that you make your own luck, and agree with McBride that there are no excuses.

Unfortunately the new-born confidence of the team vanished quickly because of the tactics used in the next match, a mid-week encounter against a combined team of Wanganui and King Country. Colin Meads was captain of the local opposition, and Campbell-Lamerton, who had returned after his injury, considered this was the moment to gain his revenge for what Meads had done to him a few years previously in the London Counties game at Twickenham. Then Meads had been his usual destructive self in the line-outs – mainly at the expense of the big Scottish Lions' captain. Mike Weston, the England centre, played fly-half against Wanganui–King Country and his instructions were to use his mighty boot to gain ground with touchline kicks. As Meads, helped by his brother Stan, won nearly all the line-outs the tactics proved one of self-destruction for the Lions, and they lost 12–6 – this after a run of eight successive victories against provincial teams. It was also the first time a Lions' team had lost to a combined side. In relative terms it was the worst display I had ever seen by a Lions' team and moved me to write for the *Daily Mail* a highly controversial comment about Campbell-Lamerton. It began 'Always bet against the Lions when Campbell-Lamerton is captain.' I went on to suggest that despite his many good qualities Campbell-Lamerton would do greatest service to the Lions by taking a secondary playing role and allowing another player to lead the pack.

Many passages of the article were published in New

Zealand newspapers. Also, Campbell-Lamerton's wife was so upset about the comments she telephoned him and expressed sympathy that he should be attacked in this way by a British journalist. In defence I argued that it was the duty of a reporter to record fearlessly what was happening on a tour. As I considered the tactics used in the Wanganui–King Country game had jeopardised the development of the team, it had, in fairness to the other players in the side, to be reported.

At this stage the Lions were building up for the third Test and it was obvious that on the evidence of the second McBride and Thomas should remain as locks. This would have meant Campbell-Lamerton left out on the side-lines. The management toyed with the idea of turning him into a prop, but this was ruined when during training McLoughlin lifted the big Scot right out of the scrum. Robins argued that they could not afford to play the All Blacks without McBride and Thomas, but conceded to the sad decision of playing Thomas as a prop. It was a costly decision because, although Thomas was strong, he lacked the technique to play Test rugby in the front row. More than this, it was an insult to the first-class props who were available for selection. So not only was the spirit of the team further upset, but the Lions' pack were pushed about during the Test and Thomas suffered a back injury. That third Test was lost 19–6, which meant the end of the series and after so many mistakes defeat in the final Test was inevitable.

For the first time the Lions had been whitewashed in all four Tests. It was a humiliating experience but a true reflection of a disastrous and badly organised tour. Even the Four Home Unions, a body hardly known to the public, felt a sense of guilt. This was encouraging, as the members of this committee were in a position to give British and Irish rugby a chance to breathe again.

35

Turning Right

Within nine months of the end of the 1966 tour the manager of the next Lions team to visit South Africa in 1968 was appointed. This was a significant move, because in the past Lions' managers had been named only a month before the team and therefore had no opportunity to influence selection or make any worthwhile preparations. More important, the Four Home Unions accepted they had failed to set down clearly the terms of reference to the 1966 management, and therefore John Robins had been prevented from having a positive say in the tactical preparation of the team – the intention and prime reason why he had been appointed. Ronnie Dawson, the former Ireland hooker and 1959 Lions captain, was appointed assistant manager and given the job of coaching the team. This was a significant move as it recognised the importance of coaching and paved the way for triumphs in the years to come.

After retiring Dawson had devoted himself to coaching, and gained respect from senior Irish players for his work, knowledge and help. Coaching was still very much in its infancy in Britain and Ireland, which meant that Dawson did not have the same advantages of Carwyn James or Syd Millar, who were to follow him as Lions coaches. A coach at Lions or national level is dependent on the quality of the players at his command, as he does not have the time to teach the fundamentals. The basic work has to be mastered at club level.

David Brooks, the manager, was a jovial, engaging character and former captain of the Harlequins. He has always been a great party man, and the Swansea rugby club greeted his appointment with a telegram which read: 'Congratulations, but who is going to manage Brooks?' The early appointment of the management meant that two men devoted to the Lions cause had a complete season to work on preparing a team. Brooks was also appointed chairman of the selection committee, a long overdue move. On tour Lions teams are selected by the manager, coach and captain. Logically, the manager and coach should have some say in the original choice of players, and the men after and including Dawson have at least had a major influence on the players named. But even for the 1974 selection the coach was not given a vote on the original selection committee.

Unfortunately the Four Home Unions have yet to suggest that the other four selectors, traditionally one from each country, should be independent of their own national committees. Often the chairman of the national selectors is appointed, which is not a sound choice, because his main concern during a season is to find his best team for the international championship. This means he watches a game thinking more about the individual fortunes of either Ireland, England, Scotland or Wales – hardly a sound basis for Lions selection. The solution is for each country to put forward men who are not concerned with selecting national sides. Preferably they should have experience of the playing conditions in the country to be visited and instructed to concentrate as much on character as football skill.

During the 1967–68 season, which formed the basis for Lions selection, it was fortunate that the All Blacks made a medium-length tour of Britain. Originally they were due to visit South Africa, but this was cancelled when the New Zealand Rugby Union decided they could no longer continue the iniquitous system of naming a team on a racial basis and leaving Maori players behind. This had happened in previous visits to South Africa, but the New Zealand public revolted at this apartheid in sport and backed this up with more than a million signatures of support.

Tom Morrison, one of the enlightened administrators in rugby and then chairman of the New Zealand Rugby Council, told me during a visit to Britain to arrange an alternative tour that the question of Maoris being excluded

37

from the All Blacks team had become a major issue in his country. 'We decided we could not ignore a million people.' Three years later the All Blacks did tour, but by then the South African Government had relented and allowed them to include Maori players. From a purely rugby viewpoint the delay was a pity because the New Zealand team in 1970 was not the same powerful combination which swept through Europe unbeaten in 1967.

South Africa's loss was very much Britain's gain, because it meant their rugby players were again exposed to the New Zealand approach. The previous All Black team had been in Britain only three years earlier and the 1966 tour had taken place in between. The 1967 All Blacks also underlined the importance of good management. They had an excellent manager in Charlie Saxton and were coached by Freddie Allen, who was then in a class of his own. Brian Lochore, a quiet-spoken farmer, was the ideal man to captain this superb team.

Under the influence of Saxton and Allen they proved that touring sides can run the ball and still win. Helped by a pack which was better than any produced by the opposition teams they successfully carried out their policy of running the ball to the wings. There was nothing fancy or sophisticated about the moves but the ball was moved at speed along the line. The only variation was the fly-half performing a loop and rejoining the line, or full-back Fergie McCormick coming in to make the extra man. Even in the final match, when defending an unbeaten record against the Barbarians at Twickenham, the All Blacks kept to their running policy and it almost led to defeat. The ball was repeatedly dropped mid-field and the forwards had to go back and save the situation. But they always believed they would win, which was a quality that British players still had to acquire.

A foot and mouth epidemic in Britain prevented the team travelling to Ireland for two matches, including an international, but the other countries were decisively beaten. Wales were the first to fall, 13–6, and this was an important victory for the Kiwis because it brought them level 3–3 with the Welshmen after 62 years competing against each other. The Welsh failed to learn from this game because they claimed they beat themselves by their own mistakes and forgot how the All Blacks had forced the errors by dictating the pattern of play. Allen told me afterwards that his team had made the mistake of overestimating Wales.

England were still going through a period of bad selection, ignored the advantages of team work learned on a summer tour of Canada, and virtually picked their side on the evidence of one game. That was when the London–Midland team put up a brave show against the New Zealanders in spite of the tragic injury to Danny Hearn. A week later eleven members of that team were selected to play for England against the All Blacks. After they had been beaten 23–11 the England selectors set about finding another team for the championship, which meant they tried three different combinations within a period of a few months. This inconsistent selection retarded the progress of English rugby.

During that tour the All Blacks fitted in a trip to France and many Frenchmen considered their well-equipped team was capable of winning. Instead they went down like the rest, 21–15, and the New Zealanders underlined perfectly in that game why the Southern Hemisphere was predominant in rugby football. During a period of ten minutes they had two scrums near the French posts and from each their forwards exploded like black missiles to force mistakes which led to tries.

This illustrated the discipline and positive thinking of the All Blacks which had been created by the superb training sessions conducted by Allen. Fortunately these were watched by a number of people who later played a vital part in the rebirth of home countries and Lions rugby. Allen was known as 'needle' due to his always demanding maximum effort from players. At the end of each exhausting session he would line up all his players and make them pass the ball along the line the length of a rugby pitch. If the ball was dropped he insisted they did it again until it was right. That was his method of teaching one of his key factors – concentration.

It is much more difficult to select a Lions team than the Springboks or All Blacks, because the Lions as such do not have the advantage of playing as a team at home. Also there is no continuity from one team to the next, and suggestions that the Lions should play matches between tours have been ignored. There is a need to encourage rugby more on the continent; games between the Lions and Europe would be a major attraction; and there would be obvious continuity if the manager stayed in control until a new man was appointed.

One of the excuses for the lack of progressive thinking in Rugby Union is that administrators, like players, are amateurs. The system often prevents the right men carrying out the work and paid secretaries are given too little power. In my experience, which covers more than three hundred internationals and Test matches plus eight overseas trips, I have met few administrators of outstanding quality. In fairness this applies to every other sport I have covered.

Among the men who have stood out are the late Sir William Ramsay (England) and Dr Danie Craven (South Africa). Sir Bill was a giant and always prepared to make a decision, a quality sadly lacking in most of his colleagues. It was a tribute to his standing that the Rugby Union asked him back to serve as president during their centenary season.

Dr Craven has an even more formidable record. Not only has he played a key part in changing rugby from a dull war of attrition to one rich with movement but he has controlled his own country's development for nearly two decades. He is also a man who will defy conventions to make progress. When the International Rugby Football Board, the world controlling body, allowed countries to experiment with no kicking direct to touch outside the 25, it was such a success in South Africa that Dr Craven considered its use should be extended. He dashed around the world to convince his colleagues but found them too conservative. However, in the end he got his way and this rule is now part of the rugby laws, and has been a major factor in making the game more attractive. I am also sure that the shrewd Dr Craven realised that this law would be a greater help to the more inventive British and French than South Africans, who tend to be rigid and unimaginative. Dr Craven has devoted his life to rugby and it is a better game because of him.

The five-countries championship forms an excellent basis for finding a Lions team, because nearly all the best players available are seen under the type of pressure vital to find the right quality. However, some countries have two excellent players in the same position and the one who fails to gain an international place is always likely to be forgotten under the present selectorial system. It is not difficult to find the first twenty-four players for a Lions tour, but the last six men can often have a major influence on the prospects of the tour.

The decision to appoint the manager and coach of the 1968 Lions a year in advance meant that two men were able to determine the type of players they were looking for. David Brooks was familiar with South Africa, as he managed a Harlequins team which toured there in 1967. Dawson's experience as a Lions captain in 1959 was the ideal background as he knew the importance of finding men with the character to stand up to the strain of a long tour. He was also young enough to have played with many of the men who were to be selected. This afforded him the opportunity to find out from his friends the strengths and weaknesses on and off the field of likely candidates. Players are often good judges of potential Lions.

Captaining a touring team is vastly different than the weekend leadership required in the five-countries championship. At the same time it is usual to name someone who is captain of his country, and the selectors came up with the ideal choice in Tom Kiernan of Ireland. He had toured South Africa twice, with Ireland in 1961 and a year later with the Lions. It is strange the number of Irishmen who have captained the Lions – six in nine tours from 1938 to 1974.

There were few controversial selections in the Lions team, when it is remembered that players unable to travel with the party were not considered. This ruled out Ken Goodall of Ireland, who would have been the best No. 8 available. The selectors made a bad decision by selecting only Jim Telfer for that position, as he had a background of leg injuries and seemed unlikely to be a dynamic force on the dry South African grounds. As it transpired the 1968 Lions were frequently in trouble at loose forward due to injuries. It is far sounder to name two players for each position on a tour and if possible opt for those who can alternate their roles.

One of the original players chosen, Bob Lloyd of Harlequins and England, was forced to withdraw due to exams and the latest Welsh wonder boy Keith Jarrett took his place. He had had a sensational debut the previous year against England, scoring nineteen points. Before the team left another change was forced. Bryan West, the English flanker, had a badly injured ankle and was replaced by the Scotsman Rodger Arneil.

Compared with the previous tour in 1966 the organisation was infinitely better, and coach Ronnie Dawson had been given a brief which put him in charge of preparing the team. It was helpful that he had played in the same Ireland team as skipper Kiernan as both men had a similar approach to the game. Not only were the first six provincial matches won but the Lions scored six tries to their opponents' one and should have been in good mental shape for the first Test at Pretoria.

Unfortunately the Lions still did not believe in themselves and this was reflected in their line-out tactics. Throughout the opening provincial matches they had adopted the orthodox eight-man line, but they decided to concentrate in the first Test on using only three men, with the giant 6 ft 9 in Peter Stagg in the middle. The short line had been used in secret training sessions but this did not help because against the top Springbok forwards and with a South Africa referee the move was a failure. Worse, the Lions persisted with the short line almost throughout the game – which indicated poor communications. At the same time it would be wrong to blame this for the 25–20 defeat. The Springboks were a superior team and only the superb goal-kicking of Tom Kiernan, who contributed seventeen points, with five penalties and a conversion of a McBride try, kept the Lions in the game.

During the build-up for the second Test at Port Elizabeth the Lions ran into refereeing difficulties – always a major problem on tours to the Southern Hemisphere, where home instead of neutral referees are used. The laws of the game are laid down by the International Board but it is the referees who are expected to interpret what they mean, and this differs in every country. The only way uniformity is likely to be achieved is if leading referees are allowed to tour like players. This would make them available to take charge of international matches and also to talk to local referees. In 1968 Dr Danie Craven opposed this suggestion and said: 'We will have neutral referees over my dead body.' By 1974 he had changed his mind – further proof that he is a man who moves with the times.

However, this did not help the 1968 Lions and their one defeat in a provincial match, 14–6 to Transvaal, was due to a dreadful exhibition of refereeing. In rugby it is considered bad taste and tantamount to squealing if the referee is criticised. One of the finest features is that players never argue with decisions, no matter how badly they might feel. At the same time as I have always considered that newspapermen are forced to be conscious of the game it is their duty to take sub-standard officials to task. Mr Koos Stander, referee for the Transvaal game, repeatedly penalised the Lions in the scrum, either for the way Roger Young fed the ball or John Pullin hooked. Young was so distressed it would not have been surprising if he had asked Mr Stander to put the ball in himself. Because of the influence of the referee the Lions repeatedly lost attacking positions and were unable to create a pattern of play.

Under the South African system for Test referees the national body name a panel of four men. Manager Brooks considered Walter Lane, who had controlled the Durban game, one of the best his team had played under and decided to ask for him to control the second Test. But Lane was not on the panel and the request was turned down. This meant that none of the original top four could be considered. Instead a J. P. J. Schoeman was selected by South Africa. Under the tour agreement the Lions had no choice, but it created a bad atmosphere for the preparation of such an important match.

With the first Test lost the Lions had to win the second to have a chance of taking the series. They played with tremendous courage in a grim defensive match and superb tackling helped to earn a draw. The only scores were four penalties, shared equally between the two teams. As feared, referee Schoeman had a dreadful game and followed the example of Stander by finding any excuse to penalise the Lions in the scrum.

Before the third meeting with South Africa the Lions met Northern Transvaal in a match often regarded as the fifth Test. Northerns fielded a massive pack and for the first twenty minutes they pushed the Lions round like schoolboys and seemed to be preparing the ground for a decisive win. Just after the start of the second half the English prop Mike Coulman knocked aside a couple of opponents when scoring from the line-out and the mood of the Lions changed. They adopted a more aggressive attitude and won, while the Northerns' forwards ran out of steam.

In the third Test at Cape Town the Lions had their chances but failed to take them, and again relied on Kiernan for their only points from two penalty goals. With the series lost the last encounter had little significance and once again a Lions team returned home without a Test win. But a lot of invaluable groundwork had been put in for the future.

Believing in Victory

Because of the anti-Apartheid demonstrations which dominated the sixth Springboks tour in the British Isles in 1969–70 the activities on the field tended to be ignored, especially in South Africa. In the light of recent events the poor results of that team should have been better appreciated. Following five major tours, with only one international defeat, they lost to Scotland and England and drew the matches with Wales and England. They were also beaten by Oxford University, Gwent and Newport, and four other games were drawn.

Even so the team received the finest welcome home ever known to a touring team when they reached Jan Smuts airport, Johannesburg. This was not due to the results but the resolution of the players to continue the tour in spite of the insults and abuse thrown at them by demonstrators. Avril Malan, the former Springbok captain who coached the team, did not receive the same welcome when he reported back to his selectors: 'They were only interested in criticising my decision to have a hooker throwing the ball in, and would not listen to my views on the improvement of rugby in the British Isles.'

Apart from the opening match against Oxford University, which was switched from Iffley Road to Twickenham to provide more protection against demonstrators, the tour generally reflected the advance of the home countries, especially in forward play and preparation. For example, that season of 1969–70 England appointed a coach (Don White) for the first time and surprised everyone by naming the captain, Bob Hiller, in advance of the team. In fairness to the Springboks they lost at Twickenham only 11–8 and were never beaten by a wide margin. Also, they suffered a number of injuries, needed four substitutes flown over, and put on an outstanding performance in the final match of the tour when they beat the Barbarians 21–12.

Before the tour started no one realised the strength of the demonstrations. To control the first match two thousand police were needed and throughout the tour the cost to the Rugby Unions and to the British Government was astronomical. On these grounds alone I cannot see the British Isles being able to invite a South African team while the present racial discrimination in sport exists in the Republic. But the South Africans can hardly complain that politics should not interfere with sport: it was the legislation of their own government which provided the ammunition which the agitators needed. Politics and sport are inevitably entwined. Admittedly the degree varies from country to country but it is hypocritical for rugby officials to say politics should not interefere with their game while they receive government support and engender national emotions by playing international matches. However, although I agree with the right to demonstrate, the players also have rights and their games should not be ruined by violence.

As coaching continued to develop in the British Isles and more players mastered the basics, so the standard of play improved. Even without the visit of a major overseas team it became obvious that the preparation of the prospective Lions players for the 1971 tour to New Zealand was on a sound footing, especially in Wales. While some officials in England, Scotland and Ireland still opposed coaching the Welsh could see the advantages and their team received total support and co-operation.

Wales were the first home country to adopt the squad system and it paid handsome dividends in the 1971 championship which they won with a Grand Slam and took the mythical triple crown. Their opening display against England in the mud of Cardiff was of major significance because it set a forward pattern which was to serve the Lions well later that year. They used the eight-man shove to such devastating effect that the English forwards were pushed all over the Arms Park and beaten 22–6.

This type of scrummaging did not help them against the

highly efficient Scottish forwards. As Gareth Edwards points out later in the book, they needed that little bit of luck to win 19–18 in a fantastic match at Murrayfield decided by virtually the last kick of the game, when John Taylor landed a left-footed penalty. Ireland were beaten 23–9 after a tremendous first half battle but the Welsh saved their finest rugby to beat a superb French team 9–5 at the Colombes Stadium, Paris. On that day even Barry John tackled.

During the post-war tours Wales have always provided more players than the other countries, which reflects their first-class club system and passion for the game. After winning all four championship matches in 1971 it was not surprising they should supply thirteen of the original team to tour New Zealand later that year, and the country's pride was satisfied by the nomination of John Dawes as the first Welshman to captain the Lions. Failure to appoint a Welshman as leader on any previous tour had been the cause of many bitter comments. Some Welshmen genuinely believed their players were considered an inferior class. I hate to believe this was the case, but in view of the background it was fortunate that a Welsh candidate of Dawes's talents was available and universally accepted. Unfortunately even the Welsh selectors had often failed to recognise his ability.

As captain of the London Welsh club Dawes had achieved some remarkable successes. Metropolitan clubs suffer compared to those in the provinces because of the long distances their players need to cover for training, but London Welsh under Dawes became the best club in England and Wales, and also the most attractive to watch. Before the new laws were introduced the Welsh had already changed their game, so their players always had support available when they ran. It was therefore not surprising that in addition to Dawes there were five other London Welshmen in the Lions team, Gerald Davies, J. P. R. Williams, John Taylor, Mervyn Davies and Mike Roberts, while Geoff Evans was one of the late replacements.

During the tour Dawes became known as 'Sid', his first

47

name, because there were so many other Johns in the team.
A quiet, serious man, he never lost his head during a game.
As a player he did not possess the exciting speed of Gerald
Davies or David Duckham, or the nonchalance which was a
feature of Barry John's game, but he had no peer as a tackler
or passer of the ball. His ability to move the ball even under
extreme pressure produced any number of tries. He and
many of the Lions had toured New Zealand with Wales in
1969, when Wales were badly beaten in both Tests. Dawes
returned for revenge. This was achieved, but he never
managed to humble the All Blacks with running rugby,
as he wished, because victory was too important. Instead
the Lions confined themselves mainly to the ten-man game
in the Tests.

Dawes became the third member of a powerful trio as
Dr Doug Smith, a general practitioner in Orsett, Essex, had
been appointed manager the year before with Carwyn
James, a Welsh-speaking lecturer, as coach. Dr Smith was a
Lion in 1950 but a broken arm had restricted him to few
games. He stated publicly that the 1971 Lions would win the
series 2–1, and was proved right, and his confidence played a
vital part in building up the morale of the team. A strong,
forceful character, his knowledge of touring proved a great
help, as he cut out the numerous official functions which bore
and upset players.

James was an inspired choice as coach. His international
career as a player for Wales was restricted to a couple of
games, as he coincided with the glittering presence of Cliff
Morgan, one of rugby's outstanding fly-halves. It could be
that this encouraged James to take up coaching and by 1971
he was ready to fill an important role in the transformation of
Lions' rugby. A major strength was his willingness to seek the
advice of players, especially among the forwards. He was
fortunate to have Ray McLoughlin and Willie John McBride
in the party, because they knew from the 1966 tour all about
the forward tactics needed to succeed in New Zealand.

New Zealanders found James diplomatic and polite, and a

striking contrast to their own famous coach, Freddie Allen, who had a rasping voice and forthright manner. Behind the gentle smile James was a strict disciplinarian, and players guilty of indiscipline during training were ordered to run extra laps round the field. Born in the same village, Cefnei-thin, as Barry John, James stood in a parliamentary election as a Welsh nationalist. After the tour he turned down an M.B.E. because he does not believe in such awards.

During the first week the team were in New Zealand the forwards spent hours on line-out tactics. They were told to forget the way they played at home, and McLoughlin showed him what was needed in New Zealand. This meant compressing the line and deliberately obstructing. It might be regretted that such tactics had to be used, but otherwise New Zealand teams would have been able to take control of the line-outs and gain valuable possession.

Those early training sessions were another indication that the 1971 Lions were dedicated to winning. It had been apparent from the day the team assembled in Eastbourne, where Ray Williams the Welsh coaching organiser delivered a brilliant talk. Williams has been a major figure in the development of British rugby. He had studied coaching in New Zealand shortly before speaking to the Lions.

All this was part of the James plan to build up confidence. As he said: 'The All Blacks and Springboks believe they can win, the Lions usually only hope they can. This attitude must change if we are to triumph.'

During the tour, when the Lions had built up an impressive unbeaten record, they were enjoying a party in Blenheim just before the first Test and singing one of their favourite songs 'We will overcome, We will overcome the All Blacks . . .' A New Zealander in the audience thought that such a suggestion was a joke and rolled back in his chair laughing. This annoyed Arthur Lewis, who threw a salt pot at the New Zealander. Clearly Lewis had got the message – he *did* believe.

When the tour itinerary was originally planned, all the

games were due to be played in New Zealand instead of the traditional start in Australia. The International Board had decided these trips should be cut in length, which ruled out a tour of Australia with the two Test matches there before starting on the hard road through New Zealand. This was a bitter disappointment to the Australians, who were fighting a hard battle to keep the Union game alive in the face of opposition from Rugby League and Australian Rules. It was therefore agreed that the Lions would play two games against the top Australian states, Queensland and New South Wales.

The Lions management had concentrated all their efforts on the New Zealand tour, and had not allowed the players enough time to acclimatise on arrival in Brisbane. This contributed to the opening 11–15 defeat to Queensland. A torrential rainstorm before the second game turned the Sydney cricket ground into a swimming pool. The conditions prevented any good rugby, but the Lions managed to win 14–12.

These games were regarded in isolation from the main tour and Barry John did not even count his eight points against New South Wales. He was only interested in those he scored in New Zealand, and they finally totalled 180 out of the Lions' 555 – six tries (worth three points in those days), thirty conversions, twenty-six penalty goals and eight dropped goals.

In the opening game in New Zealand, against Counties–Thames Valley, the Lions scrummaging impressed everyone and the 25–3 victory would have been higher if the England captain John Spencer had been able to run in more than one of the many chances he was given.

Colin Meads, the most famous of All Blacks, played for Wanganui–King Country in the second match and suffered torn rib ligaments after only a couple of minutes. Any other man would have gone off, but Meads's pride would not allow this. The last time Meads had played in a provincial game against the Lions he had been on the winning side, but after the 22–9 defeat in 1971 he was moved to say: 'This team does not believe in fairy tales like the last one. They are well organised, especially in the front of the line-out.'

Before leaving England James had pencilled in his first five teams for the New Zealand tour. It was all part of his plan to develop the side early into a Test combination, and he was rewarded with one of the most breathtaking displays of rugby, including nine glorious tries in the fifth game against Wellington. As a province Wellington have always ranked in the top flight and had known victories over the Lions, but this time they were a supporting cast in one of the finest games I have ever seen.

The Lions won 47-9 and John Bevan, the Welsh wing with the strength of a forward, scored four of the tries, one memorably, where he finished off a dazzling movement started by J. P. R. Williams near his own line. It came when Wellington were launching one of their own rare attacks. They had reached the Lions 25 when their full-back kicked straight to Williams. Strange characters, these Kiwis, Williams must have thought as he ran the ball out, linking up with Mike Gibson. Gibson then passed out to Bevan, who, running from his wing to the centre of the field and from there to the try-line finished off a movement of more than eighty yards. Accolades by the thousand were heaped on the tourists, but for James the psychological aspect was even more important. The New Zealanders now had reason to worry about the Tests, while the Lions' confidence soared. A 21–9 victory over Otago, another premier province, left the Lions ready for the 'fifth Test' against Ranfurly Shield winners Canterbury.

While the match at Wellington had illustrated all the beauty of rugby the Canterbury affair at Christchurch revealed the brutal, vicious and unhealthy side of the game. *The Times* was moved to report: 'They bayed for the blood of the Poms.' Canterbury were determined to win by any means and the punching in the front row spread to every part of the field. It ended the tour for Sandy Carmichael and Ray McLoughlin. Carmichael was pummelled unmercifully in the front row, suffering a depressed cheek bone, and McLoughlin broke a thumb hitting Alex Wyllie in one of the many punch-ups which punctuated a game soured by such taunts as 'Come on, you soft Pommy bastards.' In addition Fergus Slattery was smashed in the face when standing in the line-out, and was concussed for most of the game; Gareth Edwards was repeatedly kicked, often from behind.

The Lions won 14–3 because they did at least try to play the ball; and the courage of Bevan was magnificently displayed when he swept through two men and dived through another three who appeared to be defending their line with their fists, like soldiers in a trench. Barry John was deliberately excluded from this game for fear he might be injured. Mike Gibson played fly-half and his tackling destroyed Canterbury's favourite move of bringing Fergie McCormick in from full-back to run at the opposition like a tank.

Teams are really tested in adversity and this was the case with the 1971 Lions. During the week that followed Sean Lynch and Ian McLauchlan were transformed into Test props. For me the opening stages a week later of the first Test at Carisbrook, Dunedin, was a nightmare. The tidal wave of attacks launched by the All Blacks forwards was so reminiscent of the scene I had witnessed on the same ground in the first 1966 Test match that I feared the Lions would be swamped. Repeatedly it seemed the thin red line which represented the Lions defence would be broken, but the courage shown in resisting those attacks determined the fate of the tour.

It was also fortunate that Barry John had conversed with Colin Meads on the subject of how he dealt with fly-halves. John remembered an incident during the 1966 tour when Meads had floored another small Welshman, Dai Watkins. Meads told John that after that he had decided not to hit backs. 'I believed him, and therefore thought it was safe to hang on to his jersey as he came crashing through at me from a line-out,' said John. It worked, because even the 16-

stone Meads could not carry the 11½-stone John for long, and was brought tumbling down.

After that first mighty wave of New Zealand attacks the Lions settled down, their better scrummaging gave them more control, and John was able to torture full-back Mc-Cormick with long rolling kicks to touch. This proved to be the last game McCormick played in the series, and he must have learned to hate the name of John. Worse still for McCormick, he was off target with his kicks and could land only one penalty goal, while John collected two and Ian McLauchlan scored a try after charging down a poor clearance by Alan Sutherland. So the Lions won, 9–3.

On they went, gaining revenge over Southland, who had beaten the 1966 team; surviving a difficult game against Taranaki, and then putting on a sparkling display at their favourite ground, Wellington, when beating the New Zealand Universities 27–6. In that game Barry John scored 21 points and lifted his total after eight New Zealand matches to 115, to pass the record set by Springbok Gerry Brand in 1937. John also scored a remarkable try – by accident. There was a scrum close to the opposition posts and John planned a switch move with Gibson – but at the vital moment he found the Irishman marked, so he moved left instead of right and with a couple of jinks finished behind the line with most of the forwards still scrummaging. 'There was complete silence and I thought I had done something wrong,' said John. The applause came later, as even the crowd had been surprised.

The Lions' unbeaten run was halted at Christchurch, in the second Test. In the scrums the All Blacks pack were still pushed back but their scrum-half Sid Going kept on coming forward with the Lions flankers still with their heads down pushing. Gerald Davies had a penalty try awarded against him for a tackle on Bryan Williams, and Ian Kirkpatrick scored a sensational try when he burst out of a maul and revealed his strength and speed by beating many opponents in a 65-yard run. At one stage the tourists were 22–6 down, but they picked up six late points by running the ball as if

53

they were playing a provincial team instead of the All Blacks.

There were many, many stars on the Lions team and they left their mark in the various towns and cities where they played during the tour around the beautiful islands of New Zealand. David Duckham, the tall, elegant Englishman who replaced Bevan for the last three Tests, will always be remembered in Greymouth on the rugged west coast of the South Island, where he scored six tries. Gerald Davies, the Welshman with a razor-sharp side-step, will be talked about for many years in Napier where he scored four tries against Hawkes Bay.

The Hawkes Bay game was another ill-tempered match and the crowd showed their resentment at being beaten 25–6 by calling J. P. R. Williams a 'fairy' because of his long hair. I cannot think of a more inapt description of this magnificent player, who made such a major contribution to the success of the 1971 and 1974 Lions. He revels in physical contact and in New Zealand enjoyed helping out the front rows during training sessions. Three years later in South Africa he considered the Lions' scrummaging had improved so much that he gave up this type of training!

A tour of New Zealand is much tougher than South Africa because there are so many strong provinces. North Auckland, for instance, gave the Lions a tremendous fight before going down 11–5. It might well have been a different score but for another outstanding performance by John Williams. He pulled off a superb last-line smother tackle on Sid Going to save a try, and later made a try when he moved the ball with such speed that Duckham was given those extra inches needed to produce one of the best tries of the trip.

It is very difficult to keep teams at a peak during a long tour, and fortunately the Lions had a week without a game to prepare for the third Test in Waitangi, North Auckland. The lessons of Christchurch had been absorbed and both flankers in the second Test, John Taylor and Peter Dixon, had been dropped in favour of Fergus Slattery and Derek

Quinnell. Slattery went down with a throat infection, however, and Taylor took advantage of his reprieve to play one
of his greatest games and produce some magnificent tackling.

In Waitangi the Lions under James trained exceptionally
hard – at least all except Barry John, whose dislike for cross
country running tempted him to skip a few miles by hitching
a lift. As John was known as 'King' he was afforded a few
special privileges. As long as he kept putting the ball between
the posts, and upsetting the All Blacks with perfectly placed
long kicks to touch, no one complained.

Before the third Test the New Zealand selectors made an
important decision which was to have a strong bearing on
the eventual result. The excellent lock Peter Whiting injured
his back during training on the Thursday, and it was decided
to bring back the former All Black captain Brian Lochore,
who had retired from the international scene. Lochore was
only persuaded because there was doubt whether Meads was
fit enough to finish the match and Ian Kirkpatrick, another
prospective leader, was also suspect.

Lochore's lack of experience in the second row and the
destructive work of the big Derek Quinnell at No. 6 in
the line-out helped Gordon Brown, who had been drafted
into the Lions second row, to take the first three throws
cleanly. It was from this possession that the tourists were
able to invade the All Blacks territory and achieved a
devastating start of thirteen points in eighteen minutes. The
need for the right man to play at No. 6 in the line-out
had previously been neglected in British rugby, but it has
always been an important factor in New Zealand. Unfortunately the selection of flankers had been determined by
their role in the scrum and the importance of possession from
the line-out was forgotten. It was especially pleasing to see
the way Quinnell 'protected' Brown from obstruction, a skill
he had learned from the New Zealanders.

Edwards was in irrepressible form. His favourite blind side
break produced a try for Gerald Davies, and then from a

line-out he made a tigerish run, handing off Bob Burgess and providing a clean opening for a Barry John try. As John converted both tries and dropped a goal the All Blacks were beaten with only a quarter of the game played.

With the All Blacks needing to win the last Test to square the series, McBride realised they would be prepared to take extreme measures. He feared the game might degenerate into a rough-house, and on the eve of the Test he warned the team of his fears. It did not take long for McBride to be proved right, as in the third line-out Gordon Brown was knocked out by the explosive fist of Peter Whiting. The referee saw the incident but confined his punishment to a penalty. Such is Test Rugby, and some officials wonder why leading rugby players cheat.

McBride had been worried that, even with two substitutes, the Lions would be lucky to finish with fifteen players. He decided to create a fight and force the referee to warn the captains, so he broke up a scrum near the opposition line and finished with raised fists while Tom Lister retreated. It worked because referee Pring called Dawes and Meads together and told them to control the temper of their players. Unfortunately this had little effect on the All Black prop Jas Muller, who deliberately kicked Brown early in the second half. Brown needed eighteen stitches in his leg for this injury and a further six for the Whiting punch; he was forced to retire from the game, and was replaced by Delme Thomas.

These incidents and the tenseness of the occasion prevented play flowing and led to a game of poor quality. But the character of the Lions, which had been an underlying feature of the tour, emerged when they pulled back from an eight-point deficit. It was also intoxicating to see the joy in the face of J. P. R. Williams when he kicked a rare dropped goal to gain a 14–11 lead. However, a Laurie Mains penalty squared the scores, and the game finished 14–14. The Lions had achieved their ambition, and Dr Smith's 2–1 prognosis had been proved right. The All Blacks had taken earlier defeats well but were sour at losing the series. It was another indication that rugby had assumed too much importance in New Zealand. Yet it seemed fitting that the game's original pioneers should be back on top at a time when rugby football had entered its second century.

Pride of the Lions

'It's great to travel with you,' was Willie John McBride's favourite tour phrase; he used it to his players, the Press men and broadcasters who followed the Lions trek throughout the Republic of South Africa in 1974. *There was one exception.*

After the Lions had clinched the series 3–0 at Port Elizabeth McBride concluded his post-match speech to an audience of three hundred at the Town Hall by saying: 'I would like to mention for the first time that there has been a lot of pressure on the team, especially before the tour started. As captain I have had my fair share, and some extra has come from one British correspondent who has made a number of unfair comments before and during the tour. I say, now that the Test series has been won, that it was our pleasure.' He was referring to John Reason, the *Daily Telegraph* rugby correspondent.

The question of a footballer's ability is a matter of opinion, but the best judges of captains are leading players and opponents, and McBride, apart from being the cornerstone of the team, was considered an inspiration by his fellow players. His record as a Lions player is unsurpassed. It would be wrong to forget that when recording the story of how the Lions won, and indeed why.

As in 1971, the 1974 Lions were a well-managed and disciplined team. Some players were critical of the manager, Alun Thomas, who seemed over-anxious to please his hosts. He was also concerned about carrying out the brief of the Four Home Unions Committee, instead of using his own discretion. This made him a remote member of the party, but at least he left Syd Millar and McBride to run the team their own way.

The selection of these two Irishmen was a major factor in the success of the tour. They had played together for the

Lions and for Ireland, they were members of the same club, Ballymena, and they had the same approach to the game. They also lived near each other, and so were able to work together planning tactics before the party assembled in London.

Thanks to a recommendation of Carwyn James the team did not spend a week training on the south coast but had just a couple of days being kitted up in London, and a few days extra training in South Africa. James considered the time his team spent in Eastbourne in 1971 was to some extent wasted because players did not go flat out in fear they might sustain an injury which would rule them out of the tour.

The British Government were against the tour taking place, claiming it supported South African Sporting apartheid policies. Denis Howell, the Minister of Sport, requested a meeting with John Tallent, chairman of the Four Home Unions Committee, and Albert Agar, the secretary, in an unsuccessful bid to persuade them to cancel the trip. Few members of the selected Lions team had strong views on the apartheid laws, and realised that the tour would still go on even if one or two individuals withdrew. Playing for the Lions is the pinnacle of a rugby man's career and a rare opportunity to perform at a high standard. When I was in South Africa I questioned a number of leading rugby officials about whether the Springboks would have defied their Government in similar circumstances. My impression was that they would *not* have adopted an independent role.

During the short period the team spent in London strict security was enforced for fear of demonstrations, and two training sessions were held in secret. This had the effect of uniting the team more quickly than on previous tours. Obviously there were a number of rumours surrounding the trip, and one British newspaper published a story that the team had left secretly when in fact the players were still in their London hotel. When finally the party arrived in South Africa on schedule they were given a fantastic reception.

Relief that the Lions had arrived for what many South

Africans feared would be the last major rugby tour there did not lessen their desire to win. They believed it was even more essential to be successful to gain the status of world champions, so countries would want to tour in future to win the 'crown'. I found it impossible to explain that this was not the way sportsmen in Britain thought about the situation.

The increase in the number of overseas tours and the presence of eight members of the 1971 Lions – six were forwards – meant that the Lions were the most experienced team ever sent to South Africa. Apart from seasoned campaigners like Ian McLauchlan, Sandy Carmichael, McBride, Gordon Brown, Mervyn Davies and Fergus Slattery, it soon became obvious that Fran Cotton, Roger Uttley, Bobby Windsor and Tony Neary were to be strong contenders for Test places. Scrummaging was the team's greatest priority, and from the outset this influenced the selection of the forwards. Millar knew that unless his team could be dominant forward they had little chance of beating the Springboks. Even famous All Blacks teams had failed through the years because they were unable to master South Africa in the scrums.

J. P. R. Williams and Gareth Edwards were the only backs from the 1971 team to make the tour. In the absence of David Duckham, Gerald Davies and Mike Gibson, a new formation had to be built. Injuries upset the development of many players on tour, and this was partly the reason why Roy Bergiers, Geoff Evans of Coventry, Tom Grace, John Moloney, Stuart McKinney, Mike Burton and Tom David seldom produced the form they had shown at home.

Many Welshmen thought that Phil Bennett would suffer from homesickness and be unable to play well, yet he proved an outstanding tourist. If he had not gashed his foot scoring a brilliant try in the second Test he might have challenged the reputation of Barry John. Alan Old was in superlative form when a late tackle in the game against the coloured Proteas four days before the first Test forced him to return home. But for that injury he would have played in the first match against the Springboks at fly-half instead of Bennett. Ian

McGeechan was an outstanding footballer, and with Dick Milliken, the exceptionally strong Irish centre, formed a formidable midfield defence. By the end of the tour J. J. Williams was rightly rated one of the finest wings to visit South Africa. Unlike some in this position he was always prepared to look for the ball and scored a record four Test tries. Andy Irvine, who replaced his reliable fellow Scot Billy Steele in the third and fourth Tests, emerged as one of the most exciting of the young Lions.

As in 1971 character had been a decisive factor in selection. Thomas and Millar were veteran Lions and knew the qualities needed by touring players. These are not necessarily the same as the requirements for the international championship, and this is why many talented players have failed to produce their best overseas. In the past many Lions had been pushed around by the All Blacks and Springboks because they had the college-boy mentality. Although Mike Gibson and Gerald Davies would have been selected if available, for the first time in history the 1974 team originally announced did not include any past or present players from Oxford or Cambridge University. This was not a reflection of university standards, but indicated the current improvement in the rest of British rugby.

Traditionally Western Transvaal are the first opponents on tours, and in 1955 they had beaten a Lions team which subsequently proved to be one of the finest ever to visit South Africa. This time they were never able to challenge against the superb touring forwards, who created enough possession for eight tries. Although the English flanker Tony Neary was not among the try scorers his ability to support and feed others led to three tries. Neary was exceptionally unlucky not to be selected for a Test, only Slattery's fine form denying him his chance. After the home team had been beaten 59–13 the South African Minister of Sport, Piet Koornhoff, said it would be a different story when the Lions' opponents were Springboks wearing the famous green and gold. This only made the tourists more determined to prove him wrong.

In the second game the Lions fielded players mainly unfamiliar with altitude condition and Andy Irvine had terrible difficulties fielding the ball in the rarefied conditions of Windhoek. Jan Ellis, the international flanker and captain of South West Africa, was given too much freedom to roam the field. (In the Tests later Ellis was hardly seen because his other forwards were under such pressure they were unable to set him off on individual runs.) Nevertheless, the Lions still won.

The first anger of the tour came during the visit to Port Elizabeth to play Eastern Province, the fourth match. Something similar happens on every rugby tour. The 1971 Lions were assaulted by Canterbury and the 1972–73 All Blacks had found themselves involved in a rough game when they played their third match against Cardiff. Eastern Province were more concerned about playing the man rather than the ball and this led to ill-feeling. The Lions retaliated. Unfortunately the big crowd in the open stand joined in by shouting abuse at the visitors and one spectator threw a whisky bottle which missed Clive Rees by less than a foot. At least South Africans discovered early on the tour that the Lions could not be intimidated, and it was Eastern Province who cut the fight short.

Two South African cricketers, Geoff Deakin and Peter Pollock, the Test player, watched the game from the open stands and were appalled by the hatred shown by some of the crowd. Why had the Lions' wonderful reception turned sour? It seemed that some South Africans were still unable to forget the Boer War, and I wrote in the *Daily Mail* that this manifested itself on the rugby field. A small section of the story was immediately wired back and published in almost every South African newspaper. I was accused of stirring up the embers of the Boer War. But many members of the Lions confirmed privately that they felt the hatred of some spectators in various grounds during games.

One of the delights of touring South Africa is the continuous change of scenery and geographical beauties. The next game was in that delightful spot Mossel Bay, and the Lions put on an exhibition which, if it had been filmed, would serve as an outstanding coaching document. They beat South West Districts 97–0 and showed the control of a truly great team by never allowing the scrummaging, rucks or mauls to become loose. This normally happens in such one-sided games.

What a wonderful way for a team to build up for the last important game before the first Test, against the strong Western Province team. Springbok selectors had watched all the Lions' early matches but considered this the most important as it took place just before they met to name South Africa's first international XV. The previous year South Africa had been due to tour New Zealand but this was cancelled for fear of major demonstrations against a team chosen on racial grounds. To compensate, the South Africans ran two internal tours early in the season to find their best players, but the success of the Lions upset these calculations. Realists among the selectors must have accepted they were psychologically beaten before the series started because they had little confidence in their ability to match the Lions forward. This is something the Springboks had never faced at home before, and was a tribute to the tactical planning of Millar and McBride.

Millar knew that the Springboks would consider the team fielded against Western Province to be a shadow Test XV, and therefore deliberately included players unlikely to be considered. In fact six members of that team – Rees, Bergiers, Carmichael, McKinney, Neary and Ripley – did not play in the first Test. The Lions dominated early on, but later looked like a side which could be beaten, with the Western Province loose forwards playing exceptionally well. The South African selectors thought they had discovered a way of beating the Lions after this game, which the tourists won 17–8.

Before the first Test there was a game against a team called the Proteas, represented by coloured (mixed blood) players. Unfortunately they did not represent the full strength of coloured rugby because the bigger coloured union refused to take part as they believed such matches encouraged racialism in sport. In their view all teams should be selected according to ability and not race. This must come about if South Africa is to be accepted back into world sporting circles. It is not surprising that visitors from overseas are perplexed by the logic that the coloured and Africans are allowed to play a team like the Lions, but are banned by law from meeting white provincial teams.

If the South African Government had been sincere about their desire to move towards multi-racial sport they should have allowed the Quaggas – a team based on invitation rather than rigid selection – to include black players. The inclusion of the Quaggas on the itinerary provided an excellent opportunity for such a move. Before the Lions tour started I tried to influence the Four Home Unions Committee to suggest to the South African Board they would like non-white players to be included in the Quaggas team – but in vain.

On the evidence of the two matches the Lions played against non-white opposition a number of excellent coloured players could be developed if the black man is given the opportunity to enjoy good facilities and play regularly against top class opposition. Segregation restricts their development and it was not surprising that the Proteas team had little idea of the laws. When England played them two years previously they had had a black referee and took precautions on the assumption that he too would not be familiar with the laws. Unfortunately, the Lions expected more from a white referee, K. Katzenellebogen, but he had no idea of the off-side law and allowed the Proteas to cheat continuously. This led to Alan Old being tackled by two players in an off-side position and he was so badly injured he missed the rest of the tour.

The Springboks included six new caps for the first Test, played on a rain-drenched Newlands pitch at Cape Town, with the posts swaying in the strong wind which the Lions faced in the first half. Although South Africa scored first with a Dawie Snyman dropped goal, the Lions controlled the forward game. A penalty goal by Bennett brought the scores level at half time, and afterwards the Springboks emerged from their own territory only three times. The Lions' superiority was overwhelming, and it was surprising that Johan Claassen, the chairman of South Africa's selectors, said afterwards the game could have gone either way. This obviously did not reflect his true thinking, because South Africa made seven changes for the second Test.

After leaving Cape Town the tour moved back on the high Veldt and the first match in Johannesburg – a city built on gold and dominated by money. That was the main subject during the first meeting with the Transvaal committee on the famous Ellis Park ground. Even if Transvaal or South Africa were unable to beat the Lions, officials were still confident they would break all financial gate records and correctly predicted that the three tour games at the Ellis Park would bring in a million rand (about £600,000). Transvaal is the richest rugby province in the world and only the Rugby Union of England has more financial assets. Such is the wealth of Transvaal they were able to take scores of officials on their 1973 tour to France and subsidise more than a hundred local club officials' fares to Cape Town to see the first Test. In fact the game produces so much money in Transvaal that it is not surprising to hear people talking about professional Rugby Union being started if South Africa were to be isolated from international rugby.

Transvaal proved to have one of the strongest sides in South Africa, and the Lions were at a low ebb because of a bout of influenza which swept through the party. This partly accounted for the home team leading 9–3 at half time. It was an indication of the fighting character of the Lions – seen many times – that they were able to come back in the second half, winning convincingly 23–15.

When the Lions management were handed the names of four referees on the panel for the second Test, Max Baise, who had officiated in the first, was missing. In his place was Cas de Bruyn, who had made the headlines for abandoning a game between Eastern Transvaal and the touring French club, Tarbes, twenty minutes early because of rough play. Under the tour agreement the South African Board can nominate those they consider their four top referees and the visiting team are asked to select one from this list. It was impossible to understand how Baise could be considered good enough to control the first match and then be excluded. Lions management had not been happy about the refereeing of P. Robbertze and G. Bezuidenbout and considered they concentrated on the tourists more than opponents. Ian Gourlay, also on the panel, was not considered good enough, so it was decided to gamble on the new man de Bruyn.

On the eve of the second Test citizens of Pretoria, the second capital of the Republic, were not confident about the Springboks' prospects. They are primarily Afrikaaners who have been nurtured in the belief that rugby success is based on physical power. Grudgingly they had been forced to accept that for the first time the Lions had better forwards than themselves. This was also reflected in the South African team selection as seven more changes had been made, while the tourists fielded the team which had won at Newlands.

Under the dynamic supervision of Robert Denton, the Northern Transvaal secretary, the Loftus Versfeld ground at Pretoria has been transformed into one of the finest rugby stadiums in the world. The blue skies and sunshine which greeted 63,000 spectators helped create a scene many English cricket lovers would certainly have appreciated. The sun can often be a handicap for visitors when playing rugby in South Africa as it adds to the problems of catching high kicks.

However, it was the Springboks who encountered the difficulties on that unforgettable June day, 1974.

As Millar had anticipated the Lions scrummaging was even more formidable on the hard ground and the Springboks were soon under severe pressure and forced to retreat. This was converted into Lions points with two tries on either wing by J. J. Williams. One was converted by Bennett and the only reply was a typical Gerald Bosch dropped goal to produce a 3–10 score at half time.

Football crowds have a personality of their own and in Pretoria they are so dedicated to a home victory it is frightening. In the past I, like others from Britain, have suffered, but this time the local people were forced to witness the clinical execution of the Springboks, normally considered invincible on the Loftus Versfeld turf. In the classical manner the Lions took further control forward and completely crushed the spirit of the opposing pack. As South Africa reeled back the Lions backs were unleashed like cavalrymen and struck deep into a disorganised defence.

Anyone who watched this game would know that only a blind or bigoted observer could accuse the 1974 Lions of playing ten-man rugby. Bennett produced a performance which for most men is confined to dreams. It was his daring and courage to attack from his own 25 which produced the second Williams try and later Bennett etched an unforgettable memory when he capitalised on Slattery's ability to change direction by slicing through the Springbok defence for a magnificent individual try which had even the Pretoria crowd cheering. I never thought I would hear such an ovation for the Lions on this ground, but this tour proved that I had misjudged the people of this City. By the end the Lions had scored five tries and inflicted the heaviest defeat (28–9) ever suffered by a South Africa team. Hundreds of fans waited at the Lions' hotel to laud them. It was a gesture which proved Pretoria people could take defeat and hail their conquerers.

During a three month tour it is impossible for a team to

stay at a peak throughout. Millar predicted a low period would come if the Lions won the second Test and was again proved right. After Pretoria the team took a few days break in the Kruger Park and returned to play the invitation team, the Quaggas, at Ellis Park on the Thursday. When this game was arranged the Lions understood the opposition would include many players from junior provinces who were unable to have fixtures. Instead they faced an exceptionally strong team before a record mid-week crowd of 51,000. The Lions did not play well but scrambled home 20–16 while the crowd reacted violently and attacked the referee Ian Gourlay because it was considered he had favoured the tourists. Some spectators had been incited by views expressed in an Afrikaan broadcast heard on transistor sets while watching the game. To make matters worse the president of the South African Referees' Association publicly criticised Gourlay, a Test panel referee, as incompetent. Neutral referees must be introduced for all international matches.

Within two days the Lions played a strong Orange Free State team in dazzling sunshine at Bloemfontein, and only the Lions' refusal to be beaten kept intact that unbeaten record. During a scrum in injury time they drove with such power that a ball which had been in the opposition back row was recaptured, and a try by J. J. Williams deprived a 60,000 crowd of an estatic victory celebration. They finally won 11–9.

Returning to Pretoria the Lions met provincial champions Northern Transvaal and referee Piet Robbertze seemed to spend most of the game penalising the tourists. He ignored the Northern Transvaal tactic of deliberately collapsing the scrum and might have ushered full-back Chris Luther to fame by providing him with a chance of a fifth penalty which would have won the game. Luther failed, but it needed a remark by McBride to extract justice when Dick Milliken was fouled by a stiff-arm tackle which put him into hospital. The referee was about to award a line-out, instead of a penalty, before McBride said: 'I hope South Africa is proud of that.'

Before the vital third Test the Lions met the Leopards (a Bantu team) in an African township near East London. Although they won 56–10 in convincing fashion, the game again underlined the potential rugby talent among the black South African people. Soccer is the number one game of the Africans but the memorable hip swerve of flanker Cushe was an indication of the future to the liberal-minded South Africans present.

To save the series the Springboks had to win the third Test at Port Elizabeth, and when their selectors made further changes they included a few 'meanies' to reinforce their powers of intimidation. In the first half South Africa played their best rugby of the series and with Gareth Edwards having his kicks charged down the Lions were under pressure for the first time in a Test match. Just before half time the game exploded in a fight and McBride called the code '99' which meant his team went in punching together.

Since the Lions' tour this tactic has been widely criticised and partly blamed for the increase of dirty play in Britain. Code '99' was devised to show the South Africans that the tourists refused to be pushed around as in the past, and it avoided the responsibility of retaliation resting with one individual. Obviously the Lions were not angels but they never played the man rather than the ball because this would be against the interests of a team who set out to win. It was unfortunate that the players were often forced to fight with their fists in certain situations, but the alternative was to allow the opposition to gain an advantage by tactics designed to gain a physical superiority. Every sport has an unwritten code of conduct and this is vital in a physical contact game like rugby; but to be successful teams touring New Zealand and South Africa are forced to accept the local philosophy. It was on the 1971 tour that the phrase 'get your retaliation in first' was born. Now the Lions have proved they are no longer 'soft' it must be hoped that future tours can be

conducted without brawls or brutality. At the same time it
would be foolish to imagine that rugby at international level
will be played without the odd outbursts resulting from
retaliation for often unseen offences. It is too much to expect
the Corinthian spirit always to prevail.

The Springboks lost the fight and that under-rated player
Ian McGeechan drove them back with a lovely corkscrew
run and long touch-kick. South Africa then obliged by
throwing short to where Gordon Brown had moved, and the
Lions were given a gift try. So in spite of their tremendous
efforts South Africa found themselves 7–3 down at the interval – and a deflated side. Early in the second half 'Moaner'
van Heerden viciously attacked Bobby Windsor who was
trying to gather the ball, and what was literally a bloody
battle followed. Again the Springboks lost it and this proved
the end of the Test series for them. As South Africa forwards
crumbled, the Lions unleashed their backs as they had in the
second Test and the scoreboard spun into motion to record
another handsome victory, 26–9. Four of those points came
from one of the finest tries achieved by any Lions team. After
winning the ball from a long line-out the three-quarter line
attacked; J. P. R. Williams joined in but was deliberately
missed out so he could take a return pass from his namesake
who had struck deep into Springbok territory. The original
plan was for J. P. R. to crash through on his own but he
sensed the danger of being tackled and performed a scissor
move with J. J. Williams so that the South African defenders
lost sight of the ball until it was placed between the posts.

At the final whistle the Lions lifted skipper McBride to
their shoulders to celebrate an historic Test triumph. It had
been a hard long road over twelve years of touring for
McBride. He had known too often the painful experience of
a losers' dressing room but had always believed Britain and
Ireland had the spirit and talent to win, if properly prepared.
With Millar he had created a superb team which had won the
series in three matches by an overwhelming margin. More
than this, his team had achieved their aim in the classical

manner – crushing the Springboks forward and then under-lining their superiority with dashing back play. It was a feat which had eluded even the All Blacks, who *never* had the ability to beat South Africa forward in an away series. Masterly technique in the scrums, driving rucks, excellent mauling and a refusal to be bullied were the key factors.

Before McBride left the field he insisted on being put down so he could thank the reserves in the stand. By his gesture he ensured they felt part of the victory. It brought tears to such 16-stone forwards as Mike Burton and Stuart McKinney. Bobby Windsor, one of the wits of the tour, commenting on the decision of the Springbok coach Claassen that his players should not read newspapers before Test matches, said: 'They had better not read any afterwards now.'

It was a pity the tour could not have ended in Port Elizabeth but four more matches had still to be played and the strain of defending an unbeaten record for three months told on the team. In Durban they were held to a 9–6 lead by Natal until ten minutes from the end, but then scored 25 points in 19 minutes (including injury time).

Even with the series over it did not prevent eighty thousand spectators packing Ellis Park and paying a world record of more than £300,000 to see the Springboks make their last challenge against the fabulous tourists. Many South Africans had turned up believing they were to see the Lions for the last time on their soil.

Max Baise had returned to the Test referees' panel to become a central figure in a match of disputed decisions. Photographic evidence proved Baise was wrong to award Roger Uttley a try because South Africa's Chris Pope touched down first. Then there were grave doubts about the only Springbok try of the series because Jan Schlebusch appeared to knock on before Piet Cronje scored. Finally Baise disallowed a try to Slattery in injury time of which the Irishman gives a detailed account later in the book. My own view is that Baise ruled out Slattery's score to make up for the

Uttley mistake. Obviously he could not admit this, but told me during an hour-long chat afterwards that he saw Slattery touch down after he had blown the whistle. However, the record book cannot be changed and the final score of 13–13 meant that the tour finished with a draw, as in 1971.

Inevitably there has been a tendency to compare these two famous touring teams and this is a matter of opinion. This also applies to the opposition. The best judges are the players who appeared in both Test series and most of them have contributed to this book. Facts cannot be disputed. In 1971 the Lions scored six tries in Tests compared to the All Blacks' seven and lost one match. Three years later they won the contest 10–1 in tries and were *unbeaten*.

My own view is that the 1971 team achieved the difficult task of proving that the Lions could win overseas and this helped develop the essential confident approach which was the trademark of the next team. Millar and McBride went further. They not only created the finest pack of forwards seen on a rugby field but also provided a platform for some of the most spectacular Test tries I have witnessed.

There was little to choose between the two teams but I would opt for the 1974 side because they were that more successful at winning. And that is what sport is about.

Part Two

EIGHT LIONS

The Challenge to Rugby

SYD MILLAR

Coach, 40, Ballymena and Ireland.
37 caps. Lions 1959–62–68.

I should begin by explaining something of my own rugby career. I was fortunate to enjoy a long stint as an international player, winning thirty-seven Irish caps between 1958 and 1970, and I only played my last game for my club, Ballymena, on the first Friday in May, 1972. I was then a few days away from my thirty-eighth birthday, having played for the club since the 1950–51 season. During those twenty-four years I had the privilege of being selected for my province as well as my country and made three overseas tours as a player with the Lions, one to Australia and New Zealand and two to South Africa. I also toured South Africa with Ireland in 1961.

My first introduction to rugby was in 1946 at Ballymena Academy, where in my early years I played scrum-half, outside-half and centre. I have been able to joke to backs ever since that I worked my way up the rugby field before becoming a prop! My ambition at school was to go to sea, and at the age of sixteen I attended Belfast Nautical College as an apprentice navigating officer cadet. I continued to play rugby, turning out as flanker for the Ballymena second team. The rugby was enjoyable yet hard – and I hated it when after a match my team-mates went into a pub and I had to wait outside, still too young to be admitted.

At the end of the season I went to sea and spent four years in oil tankers. In 1955 I returned home to sit my navigation examinations, and turned out regularly for Ballymena. Eventually I won a place in the first team as a second row

75

forward. Physically I was too small for this position, but it provided excellent experience. Subsequently I was moved to the front row and played for Ulster. By 1958 I was in the Irish team and by then had given up thoughts of a career at sea.

There was a long break in my international career when in 1963–64 I was dropped. I was approaching thirty, and the selectors decided I was too old. I do not blame them now, but selectors today take a different view, as shown by the continuing career of such players as Willie John McBride and Ray McLoughlin of Ireland and Ian McLauchlan of Scotland. Tight forwards really only mature between the ages of twenty-eight and thirty-three. However, the Irish selectors did in fact change their minds and brought me back into the team in 1968, and this led to my making another Lions tour that year to South Africa – six years after my previous visit.

As my international career spanned such a long period I played with outside-halves from Jackie Kyle through to Barry John, and hookers such as Bryn Meredith, Ronnie Dawson and Ken Kennedy. Touring New Zealand with the Lions in 1959 as a raw young Irishman, in a team which included such backs as Tony O'Reilly, Peter Jackson, Dave Hewitt, Jeff Butterfield and Ken Scotland, was a memorable experience and gave me a new dimension on the game. I also came up against Wilson Whineray and Colin Meads on that tour.

At the start of the '60s the Springboks were the major power in world rugby. They beat the All Blacks in a home series in 1960 and later that year toured the British Isles and France, remaining unbeaten until the final game against the Barbarians – a game in which I was fortunate to play. My contact with the South Africans was renewed during the Irish tour in 1961 and then on a long visit with the Lions the following year. By the end of that trip I was completely converted to the importance of the set scrum.

So much, then, for the major influences on my thinking both as a player and as a coach. Pin-pointing the reason why

76

the 1971 and 1974 teams were successful, the answer must be coaching – and this is not a pat on the back to Carwyn and myself. It is a tribute to all those who contributed along the line to teach players the basics and create a climate where coaching was accepted. This was not easy, as there was strong opposition among many administrators. Conservatism in rugby football means changes are made very slowly. As a coach one also has to help the player and team achieve a winning formula without their losing enjoyment or flair; one cannot hope to put over new techniques overnight.

However, during the ten years from the mid-'60s a number of playing improvements occurred in the British and Irish rugby scene. These were brought about by the enthusiasm of coaches like Ronnie Dawson (Ireland), Ray Williams and Carwyn James (Wales), Don Rutherford (England) and Bill Dickinson (Scotland). There were many more who changed the face of British Isles rugby – the coaches in clubs, counties and provinces who often worked without any acclaim. As Carwyn James would agree, the achievements of the 1971 and 1974 Lions were due in part to the many unsung coaches throughout the four countries.

Coaching alone, of course, will not produce all the improvements necessary in rugby football. There are many other aspects apart from coaching – selection and refereeing, for instance – which need to be improved to make it a better game for players and spectators. Just as people have to be educated to become good coaches, so must others be trained to become selectors. The referee, too, has a major role to play if the game is to be enjoyed. Just as coaches should know more about the laws, so referees should have more appreciation of the game and not concentrate solely on knowing and applying the law. Rugby does not work successfully if coaches, selectors, referees and administrators are put in their own boxes. Communication is often poor between the particular parties, and the structure of the game should be examined carefully and improvements made.

Most clubs, counties, provinces and national Unions have

retained the same structures for many years, but it is questionable whether they are suitable for present-day needs. In business the methods used must frequently be examined to ensure efficiency. For example, it is obvious that the more people who are playing rugby the better it is for the game, but little is done to interest recruits. Yet at a time when individual leisure pursuits are challenging team games rugby cannot sit back and hope that schools will continue to produce players; that is not going to happen. Every sport now demands representation at schools, which means that clubs and Unions must show an interest in 'selling' rugby, especially through the mini-game suitable for schoolboys. It is imperative not to continue to ignore the value of public relations.

Many people are needed to produce the new ideas and higher efficiency which are lost because they cannot afford the time to get through the various stages of club, county (or province) and national Union representation. Ulster rugby was made to stop and think by Bob McEwen, the former Cambridge University and Scotland hooker who brought his keen analytical mind as a business consultant to bear on the game. Whatever the structure adopted it is important that there must be opportunity for people like McEwen to serve. McEwen also applied his business techniques to the game and put them together in a concise manner which has proved a great help to coaches and players.

When coaching first started in the British Isles it was said that players would become robots and teams become machines. That is the result of bad coaching, which nobody wants. I have often been accused of 'professionalising' the game. The word is used in the wrong context. Coaching attempts to produce more efficiency, but this doesn't ruin the enjoyment. When coaching is based on sound thinking it will allow *more* flair rather than less. For example, if a pack of forwards are organised to win more and better ball the backs will have many more opportunities to run and create attractive movements. And the Lions of 1971 and 1974 were successful not simply because they were drilled to react automatically. Both teams had a far wider appreciation of the total game, and their own part in it, than any previous Lions combinations. In previous tours the Lions relied on individual brilliance; in contrast the All Blacks and Springboks organised the abilities of all their players. Only gradually did we follow that example.

Travelling abroad with Lions teams over a period of fifteen years, I had the rare opportunity to watch the changing pattern from failure to success and the grand fulfilment in South Africa in 1974. That team's character and determination can be explained in one phrase, 'a new attitude'. This was brought about by the captaincy of Willie John McBride and the fine example of the senior players, and did not only apply on the field of play. Everyone worked exceptionally hard and the result was a happy and successful tour.

Lions teams are unique as national combinations because they only play together overseas. You can not ask a Welsh or Scottish nationalist to go out and play for Great Britain – or a southern Irishman come to that – so it is essential to create a spirit that is peculiar to the Lions. It is not a matter of patriotism, but more of playing for each other. A long tour has advantages, as the team are linked closely together, like the crew of a ship. If this spirit is combined with discipline, commitment and the right attitude, then the players' rugby skills can be harnessed successfully. At the same time I regret that the Lions do not have an opportunity to play at home like the All Blacks, Springboks and Wallabies.

Many people considered the 1974 Lions' overall strategy to take the Springboks on forward was unwise because they had never been mastered before. I considered it essential and, in view of my own playing experience in South Africa, believed it could be achieved. To out-scrummage them would be a psychological blow because their forwards were not used to going back. South Africans have always relied on their back row forwards to launch offensives from scrums and on the ability of half-backs to kick from set pieces. The aim was to deprive them of this advantage and ensure they worked always under pressure.

We set out to equal them at least in the scrum but managed to beat them and went forward against all the provinces. The importance of scrummaging influenced the original selection of the tour party. The Lions had to have men who could measure up to the task. I had always felt on previous tours that there had not been a full commitment from the forwards. On arrival in South Africa much time was spent conditioning forwards on the importance of the scrum on the game as a whole. It is impossible to play good rugby unless the scrum is right.

In the line-out many teams fail to pay enough attention to detail. A key factor is throwing in, but not sufficient time is spent practising this art. Fortunately Bobby Windsor proved excellent in this role in South Africa. Most teams spend a lot of time ensuring the ball is put correctly into the scrum, and that the timing between scrum-half, hooker and the shove is right, but they neglect the line-out. We could learn much about the technique of throwing the ball from American football. I once spent some time with a Canadian footballer who showed me some of their techniques. If Windsor had not been so good I might have tried them.

The South Africans spend more time than most teams on throwing. It helps that they nearly always use a dry ball, while during a winter day in Britain the difference between a good or bad throw does not matter so much because of wind or rain. In South Africa the timing of a jump is much more important.

Who should throw in the ball? There has been a good deal of argument about this. The criterion should be to select the best man for the job, provided he is not essential in the line-out or as an attacker. For this reason the choice is normally between the hooker or wing. In South Africa the Lions always used the two hookers, Windsor or Ken Kennedy. The hooker normally acts as a blind side flanker when the opposition throws in. The advantage of using the hooker is that

1. Syd Millar, seen during a coaching session, perfectly captures the professionalism and will to win which marked the Lions' tours of 1971 and 1974

The two faces of McBride

2. McBride performing his captain's task at a midmatch team briefing. Pictured with him is Englishman Mike Burton

3. As a player McBride always led by example. He frequently broke the opposition advantage line by peeling from a line-out, as he does here

the team has an extra wing for an attacking or defensive role, but it can create problems when the opposition uses a wing and your team are down to seven men against eight.

An important decision by the Lions selectors was to use Roger Uttley, the England second row forward, as a flanker. This move was considered before the tour because a hard scrummaging flanker is important and in this role Uttley was invaluable. He was also needed as a fourth line-out player and caused tremendous problems to the opposition. Rarely do you find four jumpers of the calibre of Gordon Brown, Willie John McBride, Roger Uttley and Mervyn Davies in a team, and they won the contest in the first three Tests. This gave the Lions a number of options in the line-out. Uttley is also an exceptionally good footballer, and many people forget he played No. 8 for his club, Gosforth.

The series provided many fine examples of the importance of good quality possession. During the third Test, for instance, Phil Bennett dropped two goals following scrums, the first goal after being given almost unlimited time. This was the result of all the hard work we put in on control at the back of the scrum. Edwards was thus allowed to dictate play much as he liked – as one Springbok player said, 'The only thing I've got to see him do now is light a cigarette at the back of the scrum!'

Psychology plays a major part in games, but there is no truth in suggestions that the Lions deliberately relaxed after the first twenty minutes of the Western Province game a week before the first Test to make the opposition look good and deliberately influence the selection of the South African team. A team will never get on top and then relax. Yet it was true that we tried hiding the composition of our Test team from the South Africans – and succeeded.

Their selectors misread the situation after seeing the Eastern and Western Province games, believing they could win by running at the Lions, particularly around the scrum and midfield. This was based on the assumption that our midfield defence was weak, and that we had problems in the back row. But we hid our combinations for these positions. Their selectors also read too much into the Western Province game, thinking this was the Lions' shadow team. This is not to suggest that the non-Test players did not make a major contribution, but it is a matter of getting the right combination. It is essential the back row and midfield players fit well together.

No doubt the Springboks considered that a player like Uttley needed more experience to play as a Test flanker. Our thinking was that on the left-hand side of the scrum the flanker is only responsible in defence for taking the first man who picks the ball up on that side. This means he is always working close to the scrum so you can do without a nippy fast man. Not that Uttley is slow, but he was not required to do the running associated with someone on the other side of the scrum who is normally responsible for the second man to get the ball – often the fly-half or possibly a back row forward.

Fergus Slattery, the other flanker, aimed to put pressure on the opposition for the entire eighty minutes. If the fly-half moved the ball Slattery went across the field after the centres. He has pace and immense commitment, and certainly made the Springbok back line aware of his presence. Phil Bennett has told me he would play against anyone rather than Slattery, because he will always be running at him. Slattery is also an excellent support player for his own backs.

At No. 8 we played Mervyn Davies, who is superb at the end of the line-out. When tackled he nearly always left the ball available for one of his team-mates. He is also an excellent cover tackler and worked perfectly with Uttley and Slattery.

After winning the first Test we played Transvaal, and the Springbok selectors again misread the situation. They did not realise we played Transvaal with three players – Phil Bennett, Bobby Windsor and J. P. R. Williams – suffering from influenza, all of whom should have been in bed rather than on a rugby field. The Springbok selectors tended to see games in isolation and so, when Transvaal played well, they decided to include a number of their players for the second Test.

When selecting a team you must look at the opposition's strengths and weaknesses, decide on a pattern which can beat them, and nominate players accordingly. The Springbok selectors watched Western Province, Transvaal and other teams looking for a successful winning pattern rather than giving proper attention to the strengths and weaknesses of the Lions.

I have stressed the general importance of the front five forwards but beyond this they must also have a hard, uncompromising attitude. The Lions front row, Ian McLauchlan, Bobby Windsor and Fran Cotton, refused to be intimidated. We were certainly strong in the front five, with these three backed up by such outstanding scrummagers and seasoned players as Willie John McBride and Gordon Brown.

Another key player in the Lions' success was J. P. R. Williams, who I suggest is the best full-back ever to put on a pair of rugby boots. Any kicking the South Africans did – and they have won many Tests this way – J. P. R. Williams treated with contempt. I only remember him fumbling one ball, and it was a tremendous advantage having a man like this, as the rest of the team never had to worry.

In midfield it was inevitable that the centres Dick Milliken and Ian McGeechan would be judged alongside John Dawes and Mike Gibson. They were a different combination and cannot fairly be compared. I have never seen two centres with the work rate of Milliken and McGeechan, and they also impressed J. P. R. Williams. They were committed to their job, and thanks to their strength no one broke through the middle. You seldom find players with all the gifts. It is true the 1974 centres did not have the same ability to transfer the ball as those of 1971, but they possessed other qualities which were just as important.

Some people considered the Lions in South Africa should emulate the previous team, but on tour you evolve tactics

83

and ploys depending on the players available. Therefore it would have been fatal to imitate.

It has been said that at times we played nine-man and ten-man rugby. This is true; but we also played fifteen-man rugby. In some games we played in the ten-man style for periods and then switched. The 1974 Lions in fact scored more tries than the 1955 side, who were previously regarded as the finest running team to visit South Africa. I consider we were effective and efficient, even if different from the 1971 team in New Zealand.

Obviously games did not always go as we wished but we tried to vary the tactics in each Test to keep the South Africans guessing. The first was determined by the conditions – a heavy wet ground and strong wind which made running the ball to the wings difficult and dangerous. So we used the strength of our forwards to gain possession and the half-backs generally kicked. At other times we ran the ball at the Springboks to set up rucks and keep them on their heels. South Africa had selected an attacking back row for the match and it was essential not to allow them to force mistakes and put the Lions on the retreat. The pattern of play was dictated by the weather and therefore different from the other Tests.

The second was played at Pretoria which creates problems for overseas teams because of the immense national fervour of the crowd, which usually gives South Africa a major advantage. Again it was decided to take the initiative forward on the assumption that the Lions were fitter and South Africa would not be able to withstand scrummaging for a full eighty minutes. The Lions scored two tries in the first half, and when the Springboks' forward tired in the second half and McBride let the ball run, the Springbok line was crossed another three times. This proved our plan had worked, as our forwards were completely on top physically. They had imposed their will with superior scrummaging.

Concentration had always been a key factor of the team build-up, but it was not of the same high standard for the fourth Test. The team had won the series, were unbeaten and looking forward to going home within a few days. This contributed to the problems of concentration. It is also much more difficult for the reserves to keep up their enthusiasm when they know they will not play another game. We tried hard to counter these problems and the fact that we drew, and should have won, was a credit to the team. And if we had kicked our goals in the first half-hour, the Springboks would have been trailing 13–3 . . .

Finally, one of the important factors in the success of the 1974 Lions was the decision not to have a Test team playing on Saturdays and another team turning out midweek. This is demoralising for non-Test players and makes team unity more difficult to achieve. That is why I give so much credit to the unselfish contribution made by those who did not play in the Tests, but ensured that the preparation was always of the highest standard.

In conclusion, as far as Lions rugby is concerned we must not reflect on our success but use it on which to build. New Zealand and South Africa will not sit still, as they have too much pride in their rugby. Unless we continue to develop and improve the pendulum could swing once more to the Southern Hemisphere.

Coaching – Key to Team work

SYD MILLAR

So what makes a good coach? While he need not necessarily have played at the highest level he must have a good playing background. But this in itself is not sufficient: he must have the ability to pass on knowledge.

First, a coach has to be able to **communicate** – to explain clearly and concisely *why* things should be done as well as *how* they should be done. Sadly some distinguished players are reluctant, or almost too proud, to go to coaching courses which would show them how to impart their experience.

Enthusiasm is another vital attribute. Being a coach is sometimes more frustrating than being a player, and they need their own enthusiasm to rub off on their men.

Motivation is important too. A coach must know what motivates his men. He must know them as people, he must understand what makes them tick, he must on occasions be almost a psychologist. At times players are upset by some minor trouble which would not be detected by an outsider, but the coach must understand their hopes and fears. Before the Lions went to South Africa in 1974 one noted rugby correspondent reckoned I could not be a successful coach as I had only recently finished active rugby and I would be too close to the players. This seemed illogical – for someone who has been playing recently knows that bit more about the modern game. Only a man who is afraid keeps a gap between him and the players.

Humility is another attribute a coach must have. He must *not* be a dictator, and at times must be prepared to learn from his men. No one can be an absolute specialist in every position, and there is nothing wrong in using the experience of the more mature players in the side, or being prepared to admit one is wrong.

Discipline and organisation are also essential. In his early days the coach must work to earn his men's respect. They may not always agree with what he says, but if he shows he will work himself and if he organises his sessions so that they are interesting and enjoyable he will gain that respect. Every coach should prepare his next session on paper to make sure it is positive, enjoyable and fits the need of the team. If he is not sure what he is going to do the session will be disorganised and ineffective. It is also vital to bear in mind the long-term requirements of a team.

Diagnosis and cure are crucial words for a coach, too. He must be able to read a game well and, if things are not right, to analyse what is going wrong and to correct it at subsequent sessions. Often it takes more than one session, but the fault must be corrected. And he must differentiate between cause and effect. Some people blame the backs when the trouble is that the forwards are not gaining quality possession. So there must then be a concentration on forward training. It is not only a case of what is wrong but why it is going wrong.

The relationship between coach and captain is vital, too. In the early days of coaching some people feared that the captain would fade into insignificance, while others saw the coach as a sort of captain's assistant. In fact the relationship should be a partnership – two people who think alike and who can talk over problems rationally if they disagree on something. The coach is the strategist and organiser, the captain the motivator on the field. It is the captain who has to see that ideas are transmitted from the training sessions to the actual match. Both men must be seen to be in agreement by the players. In 1974 I was fortunate in having Willie John McBride as captain, for he is a great motivator as well as an experienced player. I was also lucky with Tom Kiernan as captain of Ireland, and I know Ian McLauchlan is an excellent leader, too.

At international level I generally regard my basic work is finished on a Friday night and I stay in the background on the day of a game, allowing the captain to take over and motivate his men at a meeting after lunch. It is the captain who must make the vital decisions if the game does not go according to plan.

The game at club level is different. For a start, clubs usually change their captain from year to year and it is the coach who has to preserve continuity. A club coach may have more time with his men, but he doesn't have them through the Thursday, Friday and Saturday as at representative level. So for the club coach a pre-match talk is useful for emphasising the points he particularly wants to make and for giving him a chance to go over tactics on which the team has been working. And at any level a coach may have to reassure players and give them confidence. Some players are brimming over with confidence while others are nervous and need their coach to be present. It is also important for the coach to teach the captain to appreciate the game so he can make the right decisions during a match, and to tell him afterwards any points he might have missed. For example, he should comment on whether the ball needed to be passed, kicked or driven more.

The relationship between the coach and selectors caused some concern when coaching began. Some again saw the coach as a dictator, making the selector's role obsolete, but again it was a partnership, as one man cannot see everything. Selectors can be asked to watch some specific aspects of a game if the coach needs information or wants to concentrate on a particular factor of play. In many clubs selectors have to be 'educated' to think more about each aspect of the game, just as players do. Some men are nominated because they have been good servants to the club but have not had the opportunity to learn the essential requirements of the selector's task.

At Ballymena we sometimes had discussions where the older selectors would talk from their own experience, and that way the coach can learn too. And of course experienced selectors can talk to other, newer selectors. This exercise can provide knowledge which has taken years to acquire and can avoid serious mistakes. In all this I am not making the coach out to be a demigod, but he does have the advantage of being able to communicate both with the captain and the selectors, and his experience should enable him to look at any game with more depth than other people.

The relationship between coach and referee also merits discussion. I do not normally talk to a referee before a match other than to wish him well, but it is worth seeing him after the game to find out why players were being penalised, and so on. A coach must know the laws and operate within them. Equally, referees can benefit from talking to coaches. Throughout the world referees tend to operate a closed shop, and many are too intent on applying what are often exceptionally difficult laws as strictly as they can rather than in relating them to the context of a game. A good referee, for instance, will apply the advantage law well. In short, coaches must know the laws and referees the game.

Yet another important relationship is that between coach and administrator, particularly when it comes to the coach needing money for facilities or equipment. Of course administrators have to look at the game as a whole, but some become so divorced from the actual playing side that they appear to have lost sight of what their aims should be. Administrators must realise that their primary purpose is to serve the game, and that their ultimate purpose is in seeing the game is *played*.

In all these relationships everyone should be working to the same objective – a continual, consistent improvement in the playing of rugby football. Here, then, are the key factors to playing successful rugby. They are not intended to be exhaustive, but they are basic.

Attitude: A player must have pride in himself and a proper respect for the game, his team, colleagues, captain, coach and for the jersey he wears. He must dedicate himself to being fit and discipline himself to do what he is asked. Even a team of brilliant individuals will not perform to their full potential unless the attitude is right. This must be positive and based on hard work. Such an attitude, joined to a proper team spirit, ensures a determination not to be beaten and to achieve maximum points. So called 'varied play' can only be successful if based on basic team concepts, hard work and good communication.

Quality possession: Winning the ball is what the game is all about, but obviously the better the quality of possession the more opportunities and options provided. Good possession depends on speed and on a team going forward. Forwards must understand how vital it is to provide possession which gives the backs space and time. Equally they must recognise bad possession, and if the scrum is going backwards then the back row should pick up and drive forward. Sometimes bad possession can be improved by the speed and agility of a gifted scrum-half. The possessor is the dictator.

Handling: Good handling means having the ball in one's hands and not against one's body. It also means taking a pass early and giving it in front of the next man – and at an acceptable height. Yards can be lost if players cannot handle, yet even many top players catch and pass rather than handle. Passing a ball is a technique, but handling a ball under pressure is a skill all top players must acquire.

Effective kicking: This means knowing the areas on the field where the ball should be placed to the advantage of your own side, while creating problems for the opposition. It is essential to know *why* you kick, and your purpose. Too much kicking is aimless and happens because the player can not think of anything else to do with the ball. Ideas may range from the aim of wishing to gain ground, to vary play, to put pressure on your opponents or to regain possession from the kick-off, but some idea must exist. And remember: ineffective kicking can be punished by counter-attacks.

Gain and tackle line: To recognise and understand the effect of the gain and tackle lines is to have a major insight into the game. If players understand the gain and tackle situation they are more likely to apply tactics which will enable them to go forward. It depends on the situation whether to kick, drive or stretch.

Continual game appreciation: One must read the game's situation correctly, apply whatever tactics are necessary and also find the opposition's weaknesses. It is particularly important that the captain has a good appreciation of the game if he is to direct efforts effectively.

Concepts, variety and continuity: Spectators now expect teams immediately to produce the attacking running rugby of the 1973 Barbarians–All Blacks match. Yet the variety and continuity of that game was based on sound concepts of hard effective scrummaging and effective rucking and mauling. In other words, one must have good foundations on which to build.

Support, scan and switch: Briefly, this covers support for the man with the ball in all situations, staying on one's feet, positioning of the ball, and using the whole field, being aware of the situation, of where you can be most effective and where you might switch the direction of play.

Leadership: Often a team that looks good on paper fails because of lack of leadership or any real direction. It is important to have the right captain and pack leader, who have all the qualities of dedication, enthusiasm, discipline, game-appreciation and communication.

Defence: A positive attitude to stop the opposition and regain possession. Speed and depth in defence are important factors, and so is the ability to adapt to varying situations. It is important to organise back row defence around the scrum and to be aware that the opposing full-back may join the attack.

Selection: This should exist not only for the players but also for the coach, the captain and the selectors themselves.

These factors contain most of what is necessary for any team to play effectively and successfully.

*

Having established the basic principles it is important to use the correct terminology. There are certain words on which I lay great emphasis, and I make sure the players understand what I mean by them – 'concentration', 'control', 'support', 'go forward' and 'pressure'. I used these words at team sessions with the Lions so often that when the players presented me with a silver jug at the end of the tour it was inscribed: 'To Syd for his concentration, control and support in South Africa, 1974.' I make no apology for continuing to repeat them because they breed the right attitudes and ensure immediate communication.

Concentration covers the team, the unit and the individual doing the right thing and eliminating mistakes for the full eighty minutes. Loss of concentration can mean missing a chance or giving one to the opposition. This concentration must start in training, and requires individual and team discipline. After the third Test at Port Elizabeth in 1974 Hannes Marais, the South Africa captain, said the Springboks had concentrated for forty minutes and lost, the Lions for eighty minutes and won. It is one of the reasons I have a team meeting on the evening before a representative game. I consider it too late to instil this concentration on the day.

Control covers details like the scrum giving the scrumhalf the ball where he wants it and when he wants it. Mervyn Davies was particularly good at this in South Africa, and he and Gareth Edwards tormented many an opposition by playing with the ball at the back of the scrum. In the ruck and maul situation it's packing in a good position to leave the ball available properly for the scrum-half. There must also be control of passing by the outsides. Basically, good control means that a team appears to have more time to do things.

Support covers a multitude of stituations . . . support of the props for the hooker . . . correct throwing in for the line-out jumper . . . the wing covering the full-back . . . the forwards giving the backs ball which can be used, and the backs creating situations where their forwards are more likely to regain possession . . . and of course there is the simple interpretation of supporting the man with the ball. It also means the support of the forwards for the backs in providing the ball which can be used and the backs creating situations over the gain line where the forwards are in a position to regain possession. Key to continuity of movements is support.

Go forward because it is difficult if not impossible to play rugby successfully going backwards. Go forward in scrum-ruck-maul, etc. or by kicking, driving or running. Any other way means putting ourselves under pressure instead of the opposition.

Pressure involves finding the opposition's weaknesses and playing on them . . . pressure them into mistakes . . . pressure them by speed in the tackle . . . give them bad ball if you cannot win the ball yourself.

Keep them thinking. Vary your tactics, and don't let them off the hook once you have achieved a pressure situation (which brings us back to control, concentration and game appreciation). Before a game if you know the opposition you might pin-point weaknesses on which you can put pressure – slow back row, positionally poor full-back, centres weak in tackle for instance – and these can help to decide your pattern of play.

Fitness: The importance here goes without saying. A coach at club level has more chance of looking after this than at representative level. Indeed the national coach is dependent on club coaches ensuring that the players come to him in good shape physically. Rugby is a physically violent game and injuries are inevitable. There are many exercises which can be used to help players develop strength, speed and stamina and they can often reduce the possibility of injury, which is to the benefit of teams.

Some of these exercises have to be done without the ball, but the ball is the tool of the trade so to speak, and every moment available should be used to practise with it so that handling becomes automatic. When the basics have been mastered and players do not have to think about giving, taking a pass and when to kick, but can concentrate on the game as a whole, then it is possible to play rugby on a higher plane.

Tom Kiernan, the former Lions and Ireland captain, always insisted that sacrifices had to be made to achieve success. He is right and it is a pity that many players with ability fail to fulfil their potential because they are not prepared to give up something. Those who do adopt the right attitude discipline themselves to train hard, to get plenty of rest, to eat the right foods and to cut down on alcohol and cigarettes. In professional soccer a manager can insist on what is really only reasonable and sensible living, but in rugby it must be done by encouragement. A rugby career is short, especially at the top, and it is sad when players ponder at the end how much better they might have been if they had trained harder and adopted a more spartan approach.

I Would Like to Live it all Again

WILLIE JOHN MCBRIDE

Captain-lock, 34, Ballymena and Ireland.
63 Caps to end 1975 season.
Lions 1962–66–68–71–74. Played in all Tests 1971–74.

Compared with others, I started playing rugby late in life. After four years at Ballymena Academy, which had a reasonable record in Ulster Schools rugby, I had yet to have a ball in my hand. At the age of seventeen I had taken quite a ribbing from school-mates who said I hadn't dared to take to rugby, even though I stretched to 6 ft 2 in and weighed nearly 12 st – most of it bone. That is why I was called 'Shortie' or 'Wang' – our slang for a boot lace, long and wiry. I was accused of many things, such as being scared that I might break in two or that Mummy might not like to see her big boy hurt. In fact, I was brought up on a farm, one of four brothers and a sister, my father having died when I was four and the eldest child being only thirteen. So I had more to do after school than chase a bag of wind round a rugby field. My energy could be put to better use hogging bales of hay and straw or milking cows.

Conditions improved eventually with all sorts of innovations appearing on the land, like tractors using complicated equipment, and I found I could be spared for a couple of evenings a week. It was then I decided that I would show the 'Townies' with their big talk that even if I didn't know anything about this hooligans' game at least I was tougher than they were. I put on a pair of boots complete with those famous leather studs of the period and headed with the rabble to the playing fields – threats being hurled at me on every step. The master in charge stood in amazement, but soon made up his mind that I must be a forward since I was much taller than anyone else around. At that stage 'Forward' didn't mean a lot to me.

The practice game started and went on for some ten minutes before I got near the ball. What a stupid game this was! Then we had a scrum and after some discussion I was put in at lock and shown how to bind. The ball was put in by someone called a scrum-half and eventually ended up at my feet. Of course I couldn't resist such an opportunity and picked it up, broke out of the scrum, and hared off down the field. My big moment had arrived: no one else on that field was going to have that ball. Although very lean I was quite strong, so I lashed out in all directions at any would-be tackler. My career in rugby football was now well and truly launched. Even if I didn't abide by the laws of the game at least I discovered that some respect was forthcoming after my first appearance. My appreciation of the finer points of rugby progressed very slowly for the rest of that season, but I did make the first XV and later the Ulster Schools side.

Everything began to fall nicely into place the following season, my last year at school, and I made the Ulster Schools side again. On leaving school I worked a full year on the farm, but turned out a few times for a local junior side called 'Randalstown'. These were enjoyable days with a great bunch of lads, mostly farmers' sons like myself who let off steam on a Saturday afternoon. I hasten to add that the odd afternoon we travelled to play against the 'Townies' in Belfast the ball was usually of little importance, but much satisfaction was gained by one and all.

I well remember one very wet Saturday afternoon in Randalstown, playing eighty minutes in mud right up to the knee. It was the greatest exhibition of nine-man rugby ever seen in that part of the rugby world – I'll guarantee we played seventy-nine minutes within an area of about ten square yards. One of our forwards had a little trouble with his opposite number but the referee wisely chastised the retaliator. While this took place our player, holding two

The strategists who beat New Zealand

4. Besides captaining the 1971 Lions, John Dawes was a passer with perfect judgment. Here he turns his body into the on-coming tackler but also is in a position to give a short pass with his wrists

5. Barry 'King' John, Lions' top scorer in New Zealand, shows the concentration needed to produce a brilliant variety of kicks

Tries in dispute

6. It is the final Test in South Africa and Fergus Slattery, over the Springbok line, is about to touch down for a try—which would have given the Lions their 100% winning record—but the referee blew too soon. On the ground, helpless, is the Springbok centre, Piet Cronje, with Hannes Marais (falling, left) and Mervyn Davies (head bandaged)

7. Earlier in the same Test the Lions took the lead when the referee, Max Baise, awarded Roger Uttley a try. This picture proves that the Springbok wing, Chris Pope, touched down before Uttley (No. 6)

handfuls of the purest muck he could pick up, called 'Hey, Ref, leave him be and we'll settle this our own way.'

By 1960 I had switched from farming to banking and had joined Ballymena. My first major game was for Ulster against South Africa and I was literally frightened out of my skin. It must have been the same for the rest of the Ulster team, even more so as the Springboks were unbeaten. I was only a young lad of twenty, and was pushed and shoved all over the place – not least because they had one of the world's finest locks in their team, Johan Claassen. In that first encounter there was no doubt that Claassen was the better man, and all I could do was try to stand up against him. He was outstanding against me in the rucks, mauls and line-outs. He would use his body to come across the line, and there was no chance then of me pushing him out. He was tough, strong and much too experienced for me. Yet I never saw him do anything dirty – he was too good a player and only interested in the ball. That whole Springbok side, in fact, concentrated on winning the ball.

A year later I played in the international championship for Ireland, but I did not feel the same awe playing against the Scots, English and Welsh as when I met the Springboks. I was one of nine new caps to play at Twickenham in 1962, but my pride was somewhat taken away by England scoring from the kick-off. We lost 16–0. Somehow I survived the season in the Irish side but was fed up with the constant stream of defeats. The sad thing about selection in Ireland during the early '60s was the rift between the committee and the players. Believe it or not, I can remember a selector speaking to me just once – in a hotel – and he called me by the wrong name.

Then came the greatest surprise of my life, when the Lions side to tour South Africa was announced and I was included along with my club-mate Syd Millar. Unfortunately I had badly fractured a fibula against France five weeks before the tour. I was in doubt whether I should go, and I suppose I should never have done so. It could not happen on a Lions tour today. But I managed to have the plaster removed and to hobble on to the plane. Worse was to come in South Africa, when the teams were being selected and I could not be considered. At times I would willingly have gone home on the next aircraft. It was a good thing that I had been brought up in an atmosphere where I had to fight, because it gave me the will to go on and I ended up playing more games than many of the others.

We had a good side on that tour – big, strong forwards like Bill Mulcahy, Keith Rowlands, David Nash, Kingsley Jones, Syd Millar, Bryn Meredith and Mike Campbell-Lamerton, and good backs like Arthur Smith, the captain, D. Ken Jones, David Hewitt, Dickie Jeeps and Dewi Bebb. Coaching still meant little at home, of course, and it is impossible to organise a team properly on a tour of even four months when the basic groundwork hasn't been done. We lost the series, although one Test was drawn, but in the books we lost the tour and that's what mattered.

My big break on that trip was when I was selected to play against Transvaal, who had a number of players in the Springbok side. That Transvaal game was won surprisingly easily. I remember going into the second half and thinking how for years I had looked up to Avril Malan, the 1960–61 Springbok captain, and now he appeared an ordinary player. For me it was a do-or-die effort to make the Test, and I was fortunate to be with Mulcahy, as honest a forward as I had ever partnered.

It was after that game I realised that if only we prepared properly for tours we could get the better of overseas teams. I made the last two Tests against what was then a very strong Springbok team, but they only just beat us late in the third Test to clinch the series.

During the 1963–64 season an All Blacks team under Wilson Whineray visited Europe, and I experienced my first taste of New Zealand rugby – and Colin Meads. There was a lot of talk about Meads, who had been an international for five years and who had built up a fearsome reputation when he played against the Lions in 1959. I can remember the jibes at home from people because I was playing against Meads for Ireland. You hear all sorts of talk about threats in rugby – the usual taunts you get from people we in Ireland call 'hurlers in a ditch' – people who have never really played the game.

I had read a lot about the size and strength of Meads, but when I saw him I thought: 'Here's a guy who is no bigger than I am.' In the line-out I was marking Meads, and the first time the ball was thrown in I jumped and was knocked a couple of yards out. Picking myself up I decided this was not going to continue for eighty minutes, and in the next line-out when the ball was thrown in I thought 'this is it'. I didn't even attempt to go for the ball, but lashed out at Meads with all my strength and even surprised myself to see him go down hurt, holding his body in pain. Of course this is against the laws but was the only way I knew to avoid intimidation. Retaliation is an accepted part of forward play.

As I turned to follow play, I glanced back and saw Meads slowly getting up. He was the sort of player who would never admit he was hurt. Play went on and he never said anything, and nor did I. Some time later there was a ruck under the Irish goal. I lifted my head and the next thing I can remember was being on my knees holding my face. At first I didn't know where the blow came from or who had hit me, but I didn't have to guess twice.

After these incidents there has been no further trouble between us. I have been on two New Zealand tours and have got to know Meads very well. With the match that day evenly contested – New Zealand just won, 6–5 – Meads and I had other things to do that afternoon after we had sorted out our differences. We both knew what we were prepared to take.

I have seen and played against most of the great players and Meads has always been the man I have looked up to. He's hard in ruck, maul and scrum, and works at every phase of play. More than myself, he was a wonderful runner with the ball. He stuck the pace in two South African tours, shrugged off all the controversy that surrounded his career, and is to me the complete forward.

It is here that perhaps I should emphasise that there was never any magical three-months formula which changed the pattern of Lions rugby, as some people seem to imagine. It is true that the 1971 team which toured New Zealand was the first to win a series this century, but this was a reflection of the thinking which had been developed for some years. I personally experienced the good and bad days of the Lions over five tours from 1962–74, and to my delight lived through the changing pattern of defeats to victories. But it was a slow process over years. A number of men, mainly coaches in the four home countries, were responsible for helping our players master the essential basics to play at a high standard and adopt the right attitude. That is how the so-called 'First Professional' Lions were born.

To develop a successful team players must believe in their ability to win. When I was a youngster in rugby my first major representative game was for Ulster against the 1960–61 Springboks. We were well beaten by a magnificent team and this game had a major influence on my future thinking.

At that period British and Irish rugby was hardly organised at all, and so it was not possible to compare the forwards with overseas teams. We didn't know what we were trying to do as a unit. Individually we were as good, as hard and tough, but because we were not working together the attitude was not right. Also we didn't believe in ourselves because we were being beaten all the time.

The 1966 Lions in New Zealand were a prime example of a team which did not believe in themselves. During the tour they became disillusioned, demoralised and beaten before they took the field. On a tour you cannot afford to lose provincial matches, but this team did and frequently seemed to be doing little more than fulfilling fixtures. When playing for them I often felt isolated and forced to take the ball without any support from other forwards. Some of the backs would not tackle, and seemed to lose heart.

In my experience Irish teams have always believed in themselves – even if such belief is not founded on form! A story which illustrates this well concerns Ken Goodall, who played his first game for Ireland as a No. 8 in 1967. After a maul near our posts he remained lying on the ground but did not appear badly hurt. Noel Murphy, the Irish pack leader, turned to him and said: 'Why are you lying there? Oscars are for actors.' From that moment Goodall became a true international.

I returned from South Africa in 1962, having learned a good deal and determined to put it over to my fellow players with the help of another Lion and Ballymena club man, Syd Millar. When we first talked about coaching and organising people laughed, saying: 'What is this game coming to? You're going to spoil our Saturday afternoon. You can't have players being told where to run and when to kick.' At that stage training consisted of little more than running round a field. There was no scrummaging practice because that was considered the place where you had a rest, so you could run to the next one. Considering how this phase of the game has been developed, especially by the Lions, that attitude must seem remarkable to youngsters today. Virtually the same applied to the line-out, and I was usually the only one jumping for the ball.

It must be remembered that during this period 'coaching' was a hated word except perhaps in schools: although it had always been accepted in the Southern Hemisphere, in the Northern it was associated with 'professionalism'. Players were sometimes encouraged to think that if rugby were taken seriously they would lose their Saturday afternoon enjoyment. Obviously, at international level, team members were fitter and keener to win, but an attitude cannot be changed in a match, especially without the right training.

One important factor which eventually led to the change

of the Lions' fortunes can be traced back to 1965 when McLoughlin was appointed captain of Ireland. He created a revolution and changed the whole concept of the Irish game with his planning and discipline. The Irish team sat down before a game and actually thought out moves. For me it was the first time I was informed what they were trying to do in the backs, and the pattern of play we were attempting. McLoughlin emphasised the importance of discipline and fitness, of course. Some of the players objected, especially those who enjoyed a few pints before a match, and did not like intense training. Some found themselves for the first time in their lives scrummaging for an entire half-hour.

I have said on many occasions that McLoughlin was the man who changed Irish rugby. He was criticised but proved right afterwards. Since then Irish rugby has never looked back. Like some politicians, he was before his time and wanted to make changes rapidly – which seldom works in rugby. He insisted on having his own way, while some of the players moaned about his intense approach. These factors led to him losing the captaincy.

Before the 1966 tour to New Zealand there was a lot of controversy about who should captain the team. The two favourites were McLoughlin and Alun Pask of Wales, and it was a surprise when Campbell-Lamerton was announced as leader. This meant that from a personal point of view one of the lock positions had gone already and that I would have to fight even harder to get into the Test side. But I was prepared to do that. There was no point in going with a team if you don't think this way.

The New Zealand part of the 1966 tour was a disaster. We had walked our way through Australia, winning both Tests – the second 31–0 – but when we arrived in New Zealand our first opponents, Southland, tore us apart. Here was forward play which I respected, and I wished I could play just one game with the All Blacks. Early on a ridiculous situation arose when we were told to be in bed by ten o'clock, and that we were only allowed to drink beer at certain times.

Once you start talking to men like schoolchildren the writing is on the wall. Of course this form of discipline failed, because it didn't get to the root of the problem. The team needed its confidence built up, and the curfew had the opposite effect. What we really needed was organisation and to be told what the team should aim to achieve.

It was easy to see the management were not in tune with the players, or themselves. John Robins, regarded by the players as the coach but called the assistant manager, was unlucky because he tore his achilles tendon during the tour. Also his approach to the game was different to the captain's. And as the administration didn't seem right, so the players didn't seem right either. Some were afraid of robust play, and it was no surprise that we were thrashed in the series. But some of us came home richer from the hammering we had taken.

The way I looked at it was that if New Zealand had something to teach – which they had – then I was willing to learn. When I first played in New Zealand I couldn't believe it. I had played in South Africa, of course, but here was something different. It was a real man's game. There was no quarter asked for or given, and that was the way every game was played, wherever we went. The emphasis was in the right place – on the character of the men who played the game.

I have always thought of rugby as a game of encounter – a battle of wills. All the best Lions players feel the same, but they need to be organised so their desire to win can be united. When two teams are motivated in the same way it leads to exhilarating encounters, as seen in the first two Lions Tests in New Zealand 1971. In the first game both teams were obviously sizing up the other, with the All Blacks hell-bent to gain early points and destroy the Lions' confidence. During the first twenty minutes they launched a continuous wave of attacks and only obstinate defence and determined tackling held them out. After the Lions had hit back with an Ian

McLauchlan try the pattern of the game changed and the Lions went on to win. In the second Test New Zealand remembered the superiority they had achieved in the early stages of the first and repeated the dose. This time their will proved stronger, and they won.

Rugby encounters vary physically with different countries. In New Zealand, due to the holding conditions of the grounds, the ruck is the centre piece of the game. The New Zealand forwards have perfected a powerful drive in the loose, and smash aside anything that is in their way. Sometimes they continue even when the ball has been won because they revel in this type of physical contact. The maul, with the ball off the ground, is more important on hard South African grounds, and this produces a fierce struggle with everyone attempting to rip the ball away using arms and shoulders in a form of wrestling match.

After my first tour to South Africa in 1962 I returned home disillusioned. I knew individually we had men good enough to stand up to anything the Springboks had to offer, yet our attitude wasn't right and we weren't working together. The home countries had different ideas, and far too many players even at this level weren't dedicated to winning. Yet why were we playing other than to win? A tour reveals who can take the pressure both on and off the field. It is something you only discover when you go abroad and see the other side of men. Later in my touring career in New Zealand 1971 when I was leader of the Test pack, I said: 'I never want to see a forward being brushed aside, or pushed out of the way. At least, it must only happen once.'

Another of my mottoes was: 'Don't brood over mistakes.' The easiest way to illustrate this is to mention the former Lions captain and Ireland full-back Tommy Kiernan. If he made a mistake or gave away points he never hung his head. To him it was over and finished and he came right back into the game. That shows the character and hardness that you must have at international level.

Another story which depicts the character needed to

overcome a mistake happened in the 1974 tour during the first match with South Africa – one of the turning points in the series. John P. R. Williams made a hash of a movement with John J. Williams over his own line, and the Springboks scored a dropped goal from a five-yard scrum which followed his error. I did not say anything to either of the Williamses, because they knew they had been wrong, and little point would have been served by telling them off. Both were great players and I knew they could pick themselves out of it. More important, none of the other players said: 'Oh, why did they bloody well try to open up that ball?' Instead they went in and said: 'Right, we're going to get this ball.' We didn't succeed, but the attitude was right. I knew then that we had a side without moaners. There were no cribbers, just a determination to pick themselves up after a mistake and come back.

A more modern example of men, and of character, and indeed of how British Rugby is now usurping the Southern Hemisphere occurred during the 1974 tour to South Africa. We were scrummaging in practice before the third international, and the Test pack were not going well. I broke up the forwards and we talked, and I told them to train like a Lions Test team. The next scrummage – against our own men, mark you – was probably the hardest and most vicious we encountered on the whole tour. The pressure was tremendous, with the tight forwards determined to put everything right, so much so, that Fran Cotton lashed out at Sandy Carmichael. It was only afterwards he realised what he'd done. He was mad with himself, for he had driven his mind to such an extent that he was unable to step back but wanted to go forward. I thought to myself, 'My goodness, what a state of mind these fellows must be in if they are prepared to hit each other.'

In preparation for the 1968 Lions tour to South Africa for the first time the manager was announced almost a year in advance, but the administrators still refused to call Ronnie Dawson, the assistant manager, a coach. Yet, while we didn't win the series, there were signs that a breakthrough was on the way. Players from all four home countries were on the same wavelength, talking a great deal about scrum, line-out, maul and ruck. We lost three Tests and drew one, but it was obvious that not much was needed to turn defeat into success. I should hasten to add that at last the administration was right – a great players' manager in David Brooks, a fine coach in Dawson, who got the best out of the players, and a great captain in Kiernan, a man I had known from school days and respected very much. All the players admired him for he was an outstanding player, as good a competitor that the game has seen, and he was a players' man and still captain at the same time.

In 1969–70 the Springboks visited Britain and Ireland and were often beaten, but I am not prepared to give us too much credit for some of the results because this was a team put under tremendous pressure due to the political demonstrations. It was impossible for them to play rugby. No other touring side will ever have to endure the stresses and strains that that team went through. They still proved that they were men with great belief in rugby football, and stuck it out until the end.

Yet, even allowing for the Springboks' misfortunes, there were signs that British and Irish players were improving, especially in the scrummaging, in my view the basis of the game. Another important development in our rugby was converting hookers to believe in an eight-man shove. Unfortunately there are still many hookers who think they are a different animal to other players. They come off the field not concerned with what points are on the board but how many strikes they have won against the head. But what does it matter if you win six strikes against the head and lose the match? It is often much better to have an eight-man scrum and give the opposition bad ball than to try to win the strike against the head.

Coaching continued on the home front at greater depth and it was apparent in the home championship that things were changing. In internationals players believed in themselves as never before. They scored good tries from planned plays, but Wales were still ahead in the championship field while other countries tried to catch up.

Before the 1971 tour I wondered whether to make myself available, fearing we might get hammered again. I had seen New Zealand and was interested in going again only if there was a good chance of winning. When I was approached by the manager, Dr Doug Smith, I told him this and he proved an optimist like myself: 'Of course we're going to win.' I liked that attitude. John Dawes was the obvious man to be captain, as he had proved himself and was held in high esteem. We also had Carwyn James, who with Smith and Dawes made up a brilliant combination.

The tour was the big breakthrough – the other side of rugby for me. I had played in nine Tests with the Lions and never won once. What an experience it was to go out with three men like the 1971 management. Smith was an outstanding manager. James, a coach who got on with players, and the greatest thinker in the game I've met. Dawes, a natural leader. These three worked so well together it was unbelievable. It was wonderful to see the confidence that was built up on that tour, with Ray McLoughlin emphasising that to be physically strong certain sets of exercises had to be carried out every day.

One of James's strengths as a coach was his ability to use the knowledge of the players. With the forwards he would seek the advice of the senior men. I felt it was the right approach to get everyone involved and talking about the game among themselves. Selection of the team had been excellent, because Carwyn and Doug had travelled the length of the British Isles and made up their own minds who they wanted. It was obvious that they got the men of their choice.

Many people believe the turning point of the tour was the fifth match, when the Lions beat Wellington 47–9. That was certainly one of the big games, but funnily enough I think that the Canterbury match a week before the first Test was the most important. Beforehand Canterbury fans we met in the street were saying: 'We'll get you on Saturday.' This brought the reaction among the players, 'Well, if that's your attitude, we're prepared. We are not going to be sorted out, it's as simple as that.' It turned out to be a stupid game, and sad because we lost two players, Ray McLoughlin and Sandy Carmichael. Canterbury might have beaten us that day if they had played rugby football. They put us under tremendous pressure at times, but were too interested in punching, fighting and playing the man instead of the ball. Thank goodness we had the sense to see that the ball was the important thing. That, simply, was the difference.

The morning after the match we had a team meeting and when Doug Smith came in there was a feeling of 'What's going to happen now, with two Test players out of the tour a week before the first Test?' Smith said: 'The King is dead. Long live the King. We're still going on with the same attitude we've always had.' It was what everyone wanted to hear.

In the absence of Ray McLoughlin I was to take charge of the forwards, and we concentrated on training Sean Lynch and Ian McLauchlan into Test props. We scrummaged one day for an hour, just up and down, up and down. Players were physically sick on the pitch, but were prepared to do this for the Lions' cause. I knew then we were in the right frame of mind for the first Test on the Saturday. Before we went out on that field, I told the forwards: 'The one thing to remember is that, no matter what happens in this game, when it's over there'll be no excuses. Either we've won or we haven't. If we haven't won we're not good enough.' We needed luck to win that game, but it was exactly the lift we needed, because here was a team that had been torn apart the previous week.

I remember having doubts about that second Test because it came only a fortnight later, and we still hadn't really adjusted ourselves. On a long tour you have to produce a number of peak performances for all Test matches and I don't honestly believe we had the right frame of mind. Many of the players were not sharp or fresh enough. They had doubt within themselves. The Lions started badly and were under pressure early on. Events went against us. John Williams was concussed, we gave away a penalty try, Gareth Edwards and the back row were off form. Add all these factors together and it is easier to see why we lost our only game in New Zealand. Carwyn James came into the dressing room and said, 'Hard luck, lads'. But everybody knew that there were no excuses.

The team then picked up and hit a winning run up to the third Test. It was right. The last training session before that Test was held on a municipal ground, and there was a huge crowd, as always in New Zealand. We were messing around, and Carwyn said, 'Right, let's show these people that we're fit.' He started us running, and I think he ran us for about thirty minutes non-stop, at various speeds, up and down banks. This admittedly wasn't my strongest point, and still isn't. But I remember thinking, 'If that's what Carwyn wants I'm prepared to do it.' From that we went into various routines of play, and it was as sharp a session that I can remember on that tour.

The first twenty-five minutes of the third Test at Wellington was the finest rugby in which I have ever played. We scored thirteen points in eighteen minutes. Rugby is a funny game, and it was probably too easy. That is probably why we were mentally prepared at that stage to say, 'Right, we've done our job.' This allowed the All Blacks to get back into the game. One should never relax and allow the opposition the chance to come back. But to the credit of the Lions we showed the determination needed to hold out in the second half.

On one occasion during that game I was on the ground during a ruck, half my body caught on the All Blacks' side of the maul. Meads looked at me, and he didn't know whether to let me have it or not. In the end he snapped 'Don't be caught in that position again.' Later in the game he was caught in virtually the same position. 'Colin,' I said, 'don't get caught in that position again!'

At this stage the All Blacks became more and more frustrated, because they could not score points. It has always been my theory that if you have lost the ball, or can't see it when you approach a maul or a ruck, there's only one thing you can do and that is drive forward. That way you're likely to give them bad ball if it is on their side, or you might even drive over the ball. Either way, if you're going forward there's a better chance of winning the scrum. This happened in this game when I and two or three players hurled ourselves in and drove forward. The scrum was given to us, and Meads said to the referee, 'Oh ref, give us a break'. That was the point I felt we had them. The Lions won that match and drew the fourth, and so created history by winning the series.

I will never forget that final whistle in Auckland. At last the Lions had *won* something. And re-living it all was tremendous – after the battle of Canterbury, where we lost virtually an entire front row; the determination of Lynch and Ian McLauchlan as they stood up to the might of a New Zealand pack in the first Test; the dedication of men at last inspired to giving their last ounce in scrums, line-out, maul and ruck, never mind the tackling in defence; the cheek and confidence of Barry John, Mike Gibson – and of course the coolness and control of John Dawes and John P. R. Williams at full-back.

On the Irish scene between New Zealand in 1971 and South Africa in 1974 we had Tom Kiernan's exit from the national team, and I was honoured in taking up the captaincy where he had left off. Tom had mustered great team spirit and it was a relatively easy job for me to carry on. I admired the man and the qualities he possessed in leadership and I hope have emulated some of these. Anyhow, I had the loyalty of the players, and they all worked hard for Syd Millar in training, with the result we were rewarded with the home international championship in 1973–74 after a five-way tie in 1972–73.

I was not among those who thought that the All Blacks would disappear overnight. They are never going to be an easy side to beat, as proved when they toured Britain and Ireland in 1972–73 and won the first three Tests against England, Scotland and Wales. Then again, at the end of 1974, on their unbeaten short tour for the Irish Centenary the All Blacks underlined their ability. It is a different matter playing rugby at home, in a more amateur atmosphere than on a Lions tour, when you're living, eating and sleeping rugby.

The All Black team of 1972–73 did not have the formidable character of their predecessors. They lost more than their usual quota of provincial games, though they could usually lift themselves in a Test match. But Ireland managed to scrape a draw in the end – it was the first time I'd seen an All Black side that had scored points against us sitting back thinking they had done enough. They must have kicked themselves, because they allowed Ireland to come back and we could have won. It was a change to see this sort of approach of 'Oh well, we've scored a couple of points, we're ahead.' Previous All Black sides would have gone on to the end. I like to think this change of attitude was due to their respect for the opposition, and that they decided not to take any chances, but instead to protect the points they had scored.

When players were asked if they were available for the tour to South Africa I had grave doubts whether to accept. I was thirty-three and had already been on four tours, including two to the Republic. But I was conscious that we in Ireland had had problems over the last four or five years, with fixtures cancelled due to teams refusing to play in Dublin and Ulster. Now South Africa were in danger of being isolated for political reasons. Politics never entered rugby in my country, and I hope they never will, so it seemed my duty to go to South Africa as a player.

Another important factor was that Syd Millar, named as coach, had been to South Africa three times. He understood the problems playing there, such as altitude and hard grounds. Unlike New Zealand and the British Isles, in South Africa the maul and ruck do not occur so frequently. Although Millar was not on the Lions' selection committee he was able to use his experience to find the type of players needed, and together with manager Alun Thomas did a tremendous amount of travelling around the four countries.

In fact, the hullaballoo from various political factors never really concerned players. Everyone wanted to be on the trip. It was a great boost to know that the other twenty-nine players were interested in only one thing – rugby football – and, indeed, winning rugby football at that. I had a number of advantages, Syd Millar and I thought about the game on similar lines, so that was a most important hurdle jumped already. We were confined somewhat to barracks in London before we left and this, although slightly annoying, actually helped the boys get to know each other quicker and we got on the aircraft for South Africa a *team* almost from the beginning.

On the day the Lions team was announced I attended a dinner at Llanelli and it was encouraging the support I received from the Welsh players due to make the trip. Gareth Edwards was the Welsh captain and must have been considered as overall Lions leader, but he showed no signs of disappointment. 'We have a wonderful team and it should be a tremendous tour,' he said.

With the Welsh Lions happy and Millar as coach my confidence was sky high from the start. The roles of the captain and coach had never presented me with any problems. I have always thought the coach should be in complete charge of training and preparing players for matches. He has to deal with a team's tactical planning and to listen to complaints and suggestions sympathetically. During the 1971 and 1974 tours the captain always took complete charge on the day of the match, when his main job was to motivate. Millar was delighted that the hard core of the 1971 team's forwards had been selected, because he knew they would only be satisfied in victory. His concern was for the players rather than any other aspect of the tour, and this appealed to the team. After we had been training for only a couple of days in South Africa the English prop Mike Burton told me: 'This Millar is a bastard: he is going to make us work. But I like it that way.'

A Lions tour can be a real test of character, for you are almost professionals for three whole months: thirty men from all walks of life can get on each other's nerves in a third of that time. And then of course there is the work, both on the training paddock and in the game. As captain I had seen all the pitfalls before, so I was reasonably well prepared. I have always been a player's man, and that was my first concern. If you want the best from anything you must take care of it. The little details mean so much – like the food people prefer, the relaxation, someone's room-mate snoring at nights, noisy hotel rooms, good service in hotels, or complaints that 6 ft 4 in men can't fit into 4 ft 6 in beds. Probably most important of all is seeing that men are not too organised, and that they have freedom of speech at meetings. Group discussions were always enlightening. Having been injured so long on the 1962 tour and not feeling part of it, I always remembered to visit the sick and the injured regularly because they were *all* important.

During the week of the first Test in Cape Town Alan Old was seriously injured against the Coloured team. His knee ligaments were so badly damaged he could not continue with the tour and had to spend a couple of weeks in hospital. All the players visited him individually and then went together as a team following the victory at Newlands. It gave Alan a chance to be part of the team and join in the celebrations.

On tour I always *insisted* that any complaints, no matter

how small or stupid, should be brought into the open and aired freely. From previous trips I had seen how certain moaners formed themselves into little groups, and was convinced that if one could cope with all the problems people mentioned and if the captain could set an example which spread throughout the side, tolerance and understanding would grow – and you would have a team.

In fact I have never enjoyed any tour as much as South Africa 1974. This was not because I was captain but due to the team functioning like a perfect machine with everyone working in harmony. This obviously made the leadership easier and it never affected my own play. It was not the same when I was captain of Ulster during the early '60s. Then I did not have enough experience behind me and was unable to sum up individuals correctly. Also we were very disorganised as a team.

Knowing the men playing under you is the most interesting exercise of captaining a rugby team. Almost everyone has to be treated differently. On tour I would tear some apart verbally, while others react badly to this sort of treatment and need to be encouraged. You really need a sixth sense to deal effectively with all players.

On a tour you need thirty players but only fifteen can play in a Test, therefore there must be a lot of disappointments in selection. At my first meeting with the players I pointed this out, and told them the party is important rather than any particular team. Then there is the question of sickness and injuries which can bring about depression as players miss a number of matches and the chance of important selections. A captain must be sensitive to the feelings of individuals in these cases. Also referees tend to upset players but the team must learn to overcome this, otherwise it can affect their performances.

Before leaving the dressing room on match days I used to stress the fact that we were better than the opposition. One of the most difficult games in South Africa was against

Transvaal when we were trailing 9–3 at half time. Three of the Lions were suffering from 'flu, but I told them during the interval they must concentrate on gaining an early score. The response was superb and within a couple of minutes Dick Milliken crossed for a try which Phil Bennett converted to bring the score level. I sincerely believe one of the reasons why the 1974 team remained unbeaten was that they never thought about defeat.

From the outset the Lions concentrated on scrummaging, and the South Africans later freely admitted that they regretted having failed to maintain their previous emphasis on this art, the foundation of their success in previous years. Instead they tried to play a more open game, but were handicapped through lack of possession. In New Zealand during the 1971 tour we never had the same dominance forward, and so it was wonderful to realise how much we had improved. We were able to control the scrums and virtually every other phase of play in the Tests. This had never happened in New Zealand because our forward play had not then reached such a high degree of efficiency. On the other hand, the success in 1971 was an important factor. Yet the Springboks appeared to be beaten before they started the series, and panicked in selection from one Test to the next. By failing to continue with players they never allowed any one group to settle down as a team.

Never was the importance of scrummaging better seen than in the vital third Test when the series was won. It summed up the whole tour and was a tribute to the character of our forwards and a reward for all the hours of training. There was a scrummage on the Springboks 25, our put-in. You could feel everyone going in and saying, 'Right, this is our ball and we are going to score.' Gareth Edwards fed the ball out and the forwards took control, keeping the Springboks pinned down, unable to move. The ball seemed to stay in the scrum for an age before it was sent out to Phil Bennett, who had enough time to clean his boots before dropping his second goal of the game. The confidence of the operation was fantastic.

Before that third Test, which South Africa had to win if they were to save the series, we were told some hard men had been elected 'to sort us out'. It was suggested that in the first two Tests the Springboks had not been shown enough aggression. The one lesson we had learned in South Africa and New Zealand was that you must stand up to anything that's thrown at you. I constantly reminded the team of my philosophy: 'Never step back. We never step back, whether it's a scrum, a line-out, a ruck or a maul.' During that Test a fracas broke out which was probably the turning point of that game. We had to defend ourselves and lashed into them to drive them back some twenty yards. After this there was a scrum and you could feel every Lion saying: 'That's it, we never stood back.' From there on the game was over for them.

Motivation before the game was easy with this side because they were hungry for success. I have always believed that forwards required a little extra, because they were the ball-getters, and for this reason the pack met for a short time before lunch on the day of the game. We would go through line-out signals, moves from the base of the scrum and defence from the scrum. Then I would deal with each player, telling him what I expected from him in the unit, and that only full commitment and nothing less for eighty minutes would do. It is always important, however, to know each individual thoroughly and see with which approach he reacts best. Then the whole team would meet for a short time before we took the bus to the ground. Here it was always important, I felt, to build up confidence.

I knew we had made it when on the bus to the second Test in Pretoria we were all singing our favourite tunes, and we arrived at the ground in the midst of rendering our favourite battle song, 'Flower of Scotland'. No one moved until we'd finished.

There was a huge crowd outside and they wondered why

we took so long leaving the bus. And the South African liaison chap, Choet Vissar, who was on the bus, said after the game: 'It frightened me, you know. The confidence and the arrogance of that one incident.'

I would like to live it all again.

Line-out Play

WILLIE JOHN MCBRIDE

Before dealing with the variations that can be used in the line-out it is important to point out certain key factors.

1. Every player must know the laws. It is much too easy to give away penalty points through infringements at the line-out, much more difficult to gain them. In 1971 and 1974 the Lions players were made familiar with local interpretations of the laws, and this is vital for effective line-out work. Referees vary, and some are far more strict than others on certain aspects of line-out play.

2. It is imperative that all players can see the ball clearly, actually in the thrower's hand before it is thrown. Otherwise they cannot react properly to whatever situation develops once the ball has been thrown in. One aspect of the new law is that it does assure the ball can be seen by all the players.

3. It is vital that an understanding exists between the thrower and catcher, e.g. the height, the speed, and whether the catcher prefers to jump forward or straight up. It should be pointed out that the catcher on all occasions must bring the ball down forcefully after it is caught in order to set up a strong base on which to build the next move.

4. Support from the other players must be aggressive when the ball is brought under control. The best method of support is to try and form a wedge with the ball as an apex. Support must also be effective so the ball at all times is available for continuity, whether it is driven forward or fed to the backs.

5. I have already mentioned the cohesion between thrower and catcher but it is also equally important that all the players *know* where the ball is being thrown. This can

be achieved by various signals or code numbers with the message being quickly passed via the scrum-half to the backs. In South Africa the signals varied between hand or foot calls and the use of numbers. Even if the opposition discovers the code this does not matter so much as the importance of your own players knowing what is about to happen.

The general play of forwards, particularly the tight five, is equally important at the line-out as it is in maul, ruck or set-scrum. They must be alert, react to all situations instantly and be aggressive at all times when going forward. I have always maintained that to adopt the proper attitude a forward must never step backwards in ruck, maul, line-out or scrum. This also applies to the ball in hand – it is much easier to support a player going forward than it is to support a player running across the field.

Obviously, sometimes mistakes are made and players are forced to go back. The first aim must be to recover and go forward again. In 1971 Carwyn James used to kick the ball over the heads of the forwards, forcing them to retreat. This was good training. When Andy Irvine played his first game in South Africa he had difficulty reading the flight of high balls due to the altitude and made a few mistakes. Then the forwards had to go back and save the situation.

These days there is a lot of variation in the line-out which has never been explored in Britain before. Some points:

1. The short ball to the front of the line, when caught, is not a good ball to move, so it should be driven by the No. 6 coming round followed by the No. 7. This ball is driven – close to the line, of course, so pulling in the opposition back row – with the result that when the ball is rucked and moved the backs are not so harassed by the opposing loose forwards, and so have more room to move.

2. The ball to the middle of the line is good (a) from a controlled palm to the scrum-half who can then move it quickly, or (b) the ball can be caught and held. Here again it is important to move forward and so have the opposition loose forwards on the retreat. This ball can be driven by the

first jumper, No. 3, or No. 2 coming in on catcher No. 5. It is most important for all forwards to play their part, driving in support of the ball and catcher. Another important factor is to cover the errors equally as well. If the ball at the front is not held it is important not to commit your scrum-half, so this ball should be tidied by either No. 5 or No. 6. The ball not held in the middle of the line can be tidied up by No. 2 or No. 3.

3. The long ball to No. 7 or No. 8 can be used very effectively. Either it can be deflected straight to the scrum-half, or deflected to No. 2 or No. 3 coming round, who straighten and drive with the remaining players in support. The ball should be supported on both sides here so that the ball carrier can transfer either way when checked. This move is currently called the 'peel' or 'roll'.

The obvious variation is where the ball is deliberately stopped and rucked. The backs can either move the ball down the line or back to the blind side, the opposition forwards having been pulled into the ruck. Equally, when the ball is thrown to No. 7 or No. 8 and caught, it can be driven and rucked by supporting forwards coming round or smuggled away and peeled off the maul by the supporting forwards.

There are all sorts of variations used effectively nowadays from shortened line-outs. With two- or three-man line-outs the ball can be thrown either into the line or over the back of the line (with the scrum-half running on to it) or thrown to the back man standing off. Again, the wing can throw the ball to midfield, to a receiver, preferably a forward, who runs in from ten yards back. Lots of plays can be used with attack in mind, but the same basic principles apply to them all. The contest for possession in the air must be turned into quality possession, and every ball should be driven forward before feeding the backs.

There have been many changes in the line-out laws over my playing years, but I should emphasise that the basic principles still apply. I have never understood how in this physical forward game it made sense to separate players at the line-out, one yard between players on the same side and two feet between the lines, nor how it was possible to catch a ball thrown in straight without jumping across the line!

The key factor in line-out play is accurate throwing. Very few players, even at international level, spend sufficient time on this, yet it is a skill that can be practised by individuals.

From Mickey to Mighty

IAN MCLAUCHLAN

Prop forward, 32, Jordanhill and Scotland.
26 caps to end 1975 season.
Lions 1971–74. Played in all Tests.

When I had my first trial for Scotland, in 1962, Mike Campbell-Lamerton, the captain, thought I was a scrum-half, then a centre or even a wing. He could not believe that at a fraction over 5 ft 9 in I was a prop. Afterwards I was told that if I had been two inches taller I would have worn the Scotland jersey straight away, but it took many more trials to convince the selectors that height is not everything in rugby. I did not gain my first cap until the end of the 1968–69 season.

Now that I have played in eight consecutive Test matches against New Zealand and South Africa my lack of height is no longer considered a joke. When we arrived in New Zealand in 1971 some people laughed and others were openly rude about me and also Sean Lynch, who is not much taller. They could not believe that people of our build should be in the front row of the Lions.

Before the first game I played in New Zealand, against King Country–Wanganui, people said Lynch and myself would be massacred. I was against a giant 17½-stone prop who had been converted into the position from the second row. In the first scrum he was launched into cloud nine like a cork out of a bottle – it was fantastic. From then on he squirmed and wriggled and could not take it. However, it is better to keep a player down rather than lift him. If the opposition is forced up, it tends to ruin the quality of the ball which is won. The only advantage is psychological.

My rugby career started at the age of eleven when I was introduced into the second row of my first scrum. I played in this position in my first season at Ayr Academy, where I played all my schoolboy rugby. I moved back to wing forward in my second year at school, and played No. 8 or wing forward for the school first XV for three years, and for Glasgow schools four times. On going to Jordanhill College to study physical education I met Bill Dickinson, who later became the coach for Scotland. He told me I was not fast or strong enough to play senior rugby, and advised me to take up weight training. This was something of a shock since I had been the strongest boy at my school.

However, I followed the schedule given me, and in addition to going from 11 st 4 lbs to 13 st 10 lbs in three months I was able to handle much larger poundages. Just after Christmas in my first year of training college I was drafted into the front row of the second XV, and promptly scored three tries.

The next week I was delighted to read my name in the first XV as prop against Langholm, at the famous Milntown ground. There was surface water on the pitch, and an endless number of scrums. My instructions from Dickinson were simple: 'Push in the scrum; don't let anyone past you in the line-out; if you get the ball in your hands run straight; anything that gets in your way knock it down; tackle.' We lost, but from then on I retained my place.

My flatmate spent the whole of the Sunday morning massaging my back, which felt as though it had been worked over with a baseball bat. I cannot remember the name of the prop I played against, but I have never felt so sore after a game in my life.

From Jordanhill I won a place in the Glasgow District side. In those days I was still often told I was too small to play in the front row, and was once dropped by the district's side because I was said to be too 'dirty'! I was also criticised because of antiquated ideas such as props should not score so many tries or do such a large amount of handling. It seemed

I would never achieve my ambition of playing for Scotland, so I began to concentrate on ski-ing. I was seriously thinking of giving up rugby because the two sports did not blend together, and I was actually out ski-ing when the news came through telling me I had been capped against England. That was the end of my ski-ing aspirations.

My father was a very gentle person, but I have always adopted a ruthless approach to life and games. People often suggest I should take things more easily, but that is not for me. It must be a hundred per cent, or I would rather not play; I am only interested in winning. That is why I am so friendly with John P. R. Williams: we are on the same wavelength as far as winning is concerned.

For me rugby is confrontation, and I am not satisfied unless I am completely on top of my opponent. I never talk to a rival; if you speak to a person it is an indication he is getting on top of you. Some people threaten me, but it is silly to do so and then do nothing about it. If someone threatens you you've got them, psychologically and physically. I would rather just hit someone. I don't say things like, 'That's your last warning.' I would hit the person and tell him that is his *first* warning. Then I would hit him again and keep doing so until he stopped messing about. But I genuinely prefer not to play like this, and always try to find another solution rather than choose a physical one.

When I toured New Zealand and South Africa with the Lions I was amazed at the generally low standard of scrummaging there. They were not prepared to scrum low, and the tight heads tried to keep you up rather than making you come down. In Britain and Ireland many tight head props bear down pretty heavily. In the Southern Hemisphere they stand up just as they do in Rugby League, where the scrum is simply a means of getting the game re-started rather than an integral part of play.

The 1974 Lions tour was the first time I had played in South Africa, and I was surprised at the decline of their forward play compared to the Springbok team which toured the British Isles in 1969–70, when I won my second cap for Scotland. Then they had a big and good scrummaging side, but during the 1974 tour they were terrible or appeared so, as British scrummaging had improved out of all recognition.

It was obvious they had not been put under pressure since way back. The Springbok selectors had tended to follow the New Zealand pattern, and look more for loose rather than tight forwards – people like Frik du Preez, and Hannes Marais to a certain extent. In 1974 Marais ran about a lot, but he did not scrummage with the power he showed when I first met him in Scotland – but then it is difficult for a front row forward to retire from the game and then come back, as Marais attempted to do. The strongest prop I played against in South Africa was the Transvaal player Johan Strauss. New Zealand and South Africa tended to play big men in the front row who were good in the loose, and one prop was always expected to be a number two jumper in the line-out.

Despite my earlier comments about hitting opponents, I cannot remember any South African punching in a scrum. It was something that did not seem to bother them. Even in New Zealand it happened only a couple of times – when punches were thrown by Neil Thimbleby in the Hawkes Bay game and Jass Muller in one of the Tests. In the sense of players really having a go at you physically, the Hawkes Bay game was the worst I have experienced on any tour. This was partly due to the tactics adopted by one of the Hawkes Bay coaches. I had heard that Thimbleby was a hard prop, and considered my meeting with him a real test. Up till then there had been no difficult scrummaging, as I had mainly met wing forwards who had been turned into front row men. After the game had been going only a couple of minutes, I followed the ball and Thimbleby just hit me in the eye. 'That's one for wee Mickey Mouse,' he said. I got my own back in the next scrum, but it was not a game I wish to remember.

It was on that tour of 1971 that people in the world of rugby began to believe in the importance of the tight forward's role in the scrum. They saw how games could be won by an effective tight scrum. This was further emphasised in 1974 by the Lions in South Africa. Here as never before a British and Irish combined side took complete control in the scrum and tight phases of play, so providing the basis for our undefeated tour. The 1974 Lions' scrummaging was, I feel, better in all respects than in the 1971 tour – as John P. R. Williams will also testify: he was fired out of a scrum in one practice at a great rate of knots. He was much surprised, but also complimentary about our efforts!

The most striking difference between the 1971 and 1974 packs was in the two teams' aggression and their attitude to scrummaging. Unlike the earlier tour, practices in 1974 often had to be cut short because we competed against each other so fiercely. This attitude was reflected on the field, when no matter what combination the Lions fielded they swept all before them. Some of the opposition scrums were pushed back at a remarkable speed, and many of the props hoisted to great heights when they were caught wanting in technical skill.

Scrummaging

IAN MCLAUCHLAN

Of the many parts of the game of rugby football the scrum is the most vital. South Africa taught the world the value of scrummaging, getting their men to work so hard that the opposition would collapse at some stage of the game and South Africa would have the run of the field thereafter. At the same time they won quality possession to such an extent that it became an embarrassment.

By scrummaging well a side can control the events of a game, physically and psychologically. Yet it is amazing that so few people, clubs and even national sides, work hard enough on their scrummaging. In the Lions' tours of both 1971 and 1974 success was derived first and foremost from our complete control of the scrummage. On both tours the Lions wore down physically the opposition and then, because they knew they could win the ball on the strike position almost at will, mentally dominated them.

This success was helped by the home championship being so competitive and by all the countries sharing the same priorities. Even France has started to concentrate on its scrummaging, but in New Zealand and South Africa, where previously they had merely picked big men and had success, they lapsed into thinking that they could scrummage without practice. While this seemed obviously untrue the deterioration was not noticed until the Lions toured in 1971 and 1974. Many people still think it matters little whether a prop plays one side of the scrum or the other, or whether a lock is on the left or right. In all cases, however, the pressures and technical application of weight are so different that few players fit into both sides of the scrum with complete confidence.

IAN MCLAUCHLAN

LOOSE HEAD

The loose head or left-hand prop is the corner-stone of the scrum and must have a flat back at all times. His shoulders should be parallel to the ground or, if anything, dipped into the opposite tight head. One of the worst positions for the loose head is for him to have his left shoulder down and his right shoulder up. Such twisting means he is under pressure and not contributing to the team going forward. The easiest method to stop this twist is to bind high on the opposing tight head with the left arm, so that the arm and shoulder are rigid and difficult to move. Getting in to the scrum early and under the tight head is also a good way of taking the initiative, and this is all-important. A loose head should always attack a tight head early to wrest away the initiative and give support to his hooker. The loose head's bottom should always remain up and be as steady as possible, since it is on that that the locks and wing forwards must push. That way they can apply weight readily and efficiently and so lend most support to the props and hooker. Usually, if the prop's bottom moves you find that he is in trouble, and he cannot be helped. The second row and wing forward have no stable base on which to push and the rot sets in from front to back. The loose head should at all times stay close to the hooker on his own ball by pulling strongly on the right arm, and on the opposition ball by pushing in and forward, pushing the hips across the scrum.

If his hooker strikes against the head the loose head should push his hip into the scrum and allow the hooker to lean heavily on him. Some hookers do not like a tight arm bind when going against the head, but at no time must the front row binding be slack enough to be broken or as to allow the second row to slip through between the hooker and the prop. On an eight-man push the loose head's binding should be as tight as possible, as should his grip on the opposition tight head. The loose head should stay close to his opposite number so that he can attack at all times.

The method used by New Zealand and South Africa – of the loose head standing out – is lazy and ineffective. No pressure can be put on the opposition tight head, who can therefore strike for the ball without fear of being lifted or pushed back, as there is no one directly opposite him in the scrum. At the same time, the opposing tight head can put pressure on the hooker, as there is space between the hooker's hips and the loose head's. This affects the second row push and the whole forward effort. Much of the Lions' success in pushing South Africa was because of the way we propped.

The foot position used by the loose head depends on his individual strength. The method that I advocate and many other loose head props favour is standing actually behind the hooker in a wide-stride position, the left foot slightly in advance of the right, the right itself solid into the scrum; both knees flexed, hips up, head up and back flat. This method of propping allows the hooker to come across towards the mouth of the tunnel. It tightens the bind between the hooker and the loose head, and also allows them to offset much of the pressure on the hooker from the opposing tight head side. It means that the hooker is much nearer the ball; and if he turns his hips the second row can slip his head behind the hooker: the hooker is never obstructed in going for the ball by the second row's head. Another advantage of the wide-stride position is that it immediately opens up a wide 'Channel One' for the hooker to strike the ball back.

THE HOOKER

The hooker's principal job is to win his own ball cleanly without upsetting the rest of the scrummaging unit. A hooker who crawls and swings and dips and lowers often wins the ball but he can make the rest of the pack so uncomfortable that he is more of a liability than an asset. On his own ball the hooker should take up position as close to the mouth of the tunnel as possible. By binding firmly on the loose head and not so hard on the tight head he can swing or open his hips towards the ball. He can also drop his right shoulder into his opposite number's neck, or dip in so that the opposing hooker is pushed further away from the ball at the put-in. The hooker should bear his weight on one leg, preferably the left, to allow the right leg free for hooking. The lower the scrum the further back the hooker has to take his feet so an optimum height is needed at which to strike and push. If positioned too low he cannot strike freely, and if too high he is exposed to the strike by the opposing tight head prop, while the push by the other forwards is wasted. Every team must adjust the right height for themselves.

A hooker is put under pressure when
(a) the opposition tight head is better than his own loose head;
(b) the opposition hooker has a faster strike; and when
(c) the scrum is so low that he cannot strike.

When the opposing tight head is giving the loose head a torrid afternoon and obviously has the upper hand the hooker can do two things. First, he can underbind on the loose head: this takes pressure off himself while at the same time it allows the loose head to move up and further under the opposing tight head, so giving him a better chance to offset the pressure put on him. Second, he can move across nearer his own tight head, thus helping to prop him up. He would here strike with his left foot. There is a third method, now made illegal, that of nodding the ball back with the head, a favourite with many hookers, not least Bobby 'The Duke' Windsor who astounded many South Africans with his ability in this department!

A hooker can also put pressure on his opposite number by
(a) beating him to the strike – highly unlikely in most international matches these days;
(b) bearing down on him with the shoulder;
(c) slipping under him and lifting him up.

Method (a) is mainly an element of surprise. Hookers like John Pullin and Ken Kennedy are past-masters of this art. They try a few strikes against the head early in the game, attempting to upset their opposite number; if they get one they may try a few more, or just forget it. Then suddenly, within crucial areas of the field, like either 25, these wily characters will snake out to win a vital head. Pullin and Kennedy of course are exceptional strikers, and can time their strikes to perfection. The hooker who strikes against the head all the time often does more harm to his own side than to the opposition. His dipping for the ball does not allow the second row a proper drive, and by striking he puts no physical pressure on the opposite pack.

Method (b), in which one puts pressure on the opposition hooker physically, may not win all that many strikes, but it can do untold damage to the quality possession gained by the opposition. A hooker under physical pressure often does not strike the ball cleanly, thus denying attacking ball to the opposition.

(c) The hooker who is prepared to play as an extra prop often helps the whole eight to function as a better scrummage unit in the eight-man drives, helping to tire the opposition or at least making them fight very hard for possession. The ideal, of course, is to mix up the two methods (a) and (b): sometimes striking, sometimes eight-manning, so that the opposition are being constantly asked questions and are not allowed to settle to one method of winning the ball. I would qualify that again by saying that if you are causing havoc by eight-manning then eight-man the whole game; just as if your hooker was winning easily on the strike then strike all the game. Whichever method works best in each game, use it to the full advantage.

Talking of pushing the whole game reminds me of when we played Wairarapa–Bush in 1971. Frank Laidlaw was leading the pack and, being a great advocate of the eight-man push, called for it time and again. Towards half time, when there had been a quick succession of scrums, he again shouted for the eight-man push. There was a plaintive cry from the second row from a very tired lock-forward named Gordon Brown, 'Push yer sel'.'

TIGHT HEAD PROP

Many people would argue that the tight head prop holds the key to a good scrum. When it is the opponent's ball he is being disruptive; on his own ball, the opposing loose head is trying to work on him. The tight head is certainly a great influence in any scrum. The basic job is to support the hooker and to provide a platform for the second row and wing forwards to push.

In my opinion the tight head should never strike for the ball, as he is for a moment on one foot and so extremely vulnerable to being lifted or pushed back. At all times the tight forward should stay straight, never angle in on the hooker. Such angling in exposes the tight head to being twisted or pulled out of the scrum by the opposition loose head. It also makes it difficult for his second row to apply weight and therefore disrupts the whole unit for no real gain. In South Africa the main tactic used by their tight head was to pull down an opponent's jersey (this is not allowed in Britain) while the Lions' main tight head tactic was to draw in the South African loose head and pull the scrum down low, so making the strike very difficult. With three such huge and exceptionally strong men as Sandy Carmichael, Fran Cotton, and Mike Burton it was found that in all games this tactic paid huge dividends, since the effort of holding them up proved too much for most of the South African loose heads.

THE TWO LOCKS

The locks, or second row, are the power unit of the scrum and are generally the biggest and heaviest men in the side. These two contribute the most forward drive in the scrum. The prop is only as good as his second row and flanker, as many a prop will tell you. Without good locks scrummaging is an arduous task. The second row should have their feet spread wide and in line, so that they have a wide base. This position also serves to stabilise the scrum and stop it wheeling from side to side. The outside foot should be slightly in advance of the inside one, the knees bent and ready to straighten and drive when the ball comes into the scrum. The back should be flat with the bottom slightly higher than the shoulders. The two locks must be linked tightly and present a good area for the No. 8 to push on. The locks outside bind through the props' legs and lift their arms as high on to the waistbands of the shorts as possible. This enables the lock to work in the inner muscle range – a very strong position. It allows the prop to have his outside leg unhindered to make minor adjustments, and gives the wing forward a much clearer area on which to apply his push. On the put-in on his own ball the left side lock has the difficult job of fitting in with the hooker sitting across the prop. There is then no gap for him to put his head through, so he has to apply all his push to the loose head and must keep his head behind the hooker. This is made easier by the hooker turning his hips, as I have already explained.

This sounds a most uncomfortable and unlikely position from which to operate, but in practice it is very easy, and is the method of scrummaging employed by most international packs at present. Gordon Brown, who is the best scrummager I have ever had behind me, finds the position comfortable to play and easy to adopt, and the fact that all his weight is on the prop means that the hooker can dip as much as he likes without affecting the second row position. On the opposition put-in, of course, the left second row's head does come through between the loose head and the hooker into what might be termed the 'more natural' position. When the hooker strikes against the head the loose head must follow the hooker across the tunnel with his hips so that, when the strike is made, the lock has the prop's hips on which to push and not a hole into which he will fall forward. Too often the loose head is guilty of parting from his hooker on the opposition ball.

FLANKERS

The modern flanker is expected to push his full weight in the scrum as well as doing all the running, harrassing and counter-attacking that has always been his role. In the two most recent Lions tours different roles have been expected of the right and left side wing forwards, with the right side being the loose, wide ranging player and the left side taking on the immediate defence around the periphery of the scrum – for instance, the responsibility for dealing with a break by the opposing No. 8 or scrum-half. The importance of flankers is alignment of force – his contribution pound for pound is as great as that of the locks.

The selection of contrasting players as flankers was adopted by the Springboks, who played Johan Kutzinger, normally a lock, at wing forward as the Lions have done so successfully with Roger Uttley. The contrast and style of Uttley and Fergus Slattery, plus Uttley's weight and strength in supporting the loose head side of the scrum, added power to the Lions pack.

Another task for the left side wing forward is to channel the ball across the scrum if the scrum-half is in trouble and the heel down Channel One is slow. It is the wing forward who does this job because he is in a better position to do so than the lock, who is bearing the brunt of the opposition's push.

THE NO. 8

The No. 8 is the back man of the scrum and draws it all together. He has the dual role of tight forward and loose forward in that he is worked very hard in the set-piece and yet still must do his share in the immediate defence in close counter-attack near the scrum. It is also the No. 8 who channels the ball into the space to his right and provides the cover for the scrum-half. In the set-scrum No. 8 pushes in the same way as the locks, with his feet spread wide, flat on the ground, head up, hips up, back flat and knees flexed ready to push through. He binds round the locks and draws them together. Again a tight bind is necessary. When the ball is won the No. 8 and scrum-half combine to decide whether it is channelled or lifted and driven.

One of the most important tasks of the No. 8 is the control at the back of the scrum. This was one of the Lions' strengths in 1971-74 in that in Mervyn Davies we had a player who controls the ball easily and drives strongly from the scrum. As is perhaps best shown if ever the scrum is wheeled, Mervyn always seems to do something constructive, and never leaves his scrum-half to sort out any difficult situation or bad ball.

In the case of flankers the feet are spread wide to give good balance and a base for a powerful drive forward. The outside foot is always slightly in advance of the inside to give stability and a more powerful driving position. The wide stance stops the scrum wheeling round before the ball comes in, and gives a very wide channel through which the ball can pass easily. Note slight angling in of the wing forwards. For the left side it is (a) to keep Channel One open as much as possible; (b) to protect the scrum-half if the ball is struck down Channel One by pushing the hips out and forcing the opposition scrum-half to run round the hips, and thus give more time to your own team; (c) the left flanker is the man responsible for channelling ball across, and so is in good position to do so with his right foot. For the right side it is to help push the tight head prop across the scrum and his angling in also stops any lateral movement of the scrummage.

The angle at which these players push should be slight, since their main effort should always be forward. At no time should any other player in the scrum push at an angle; it is a waste of effort and is disruptive and uncomfortable for his colleagues. Not at any time should the scrum go down with less than five people bound together. Having five at once helps to stabilise the scrum, and if the opposition go down in ones and twos then they lose the initiative and the tight bind of an organised unit.

There should be as little movement of feet as possible after the enemy are engaged, and all concentration should be on the explosive effort forward. Everyone's head should be up, to help maintain a straight back, and also where possible to see the ball. As any hooker will tell you, it is infinitely easier to win ball going forward than it is standing still or going back. As the ball comes in the front row should lift up slightly and forward on to the ball, making the hooker's strike easy and controlled. At the same time it sets the opposition hooker back, cancelling his attempt to take the strike.

All this is only possible if everything functions properly. A full list reads:

Players' position; balance; poise; tight binding; flexed legs
Alertness; timing; attitude
Application and good ball.

Channel 1

Where the ball is struck through the prop and lock's legs, and out between the left flanker and No. 8. This is a quick, clean, in-and-out ball to give the scrum-half the fastest possession possible to get line moving. It is a good ball to get if the other side are putting you under severe pressure by pushing or wheeling. Channel One ball must never be slow, since this would allow the opposing scrum-half too much time to exert pressure on your scrum-half.

Channel 2

A controlled ball which can be held by the No. 8, to be picked and driven or pulled across to the right for the scrum-half to use without being under pressure from his opposite number or wing forwards. This ball can only be used effectively if the scrum is moving forward and the ball is well controlled.

This ball can be struck through by the hooker or pushed across by the left flanker or No. 8.

Again it is a good tactic to mix both Channel One and Two balls to keep the opposition guessing, or to draw them offside. A favourite play of Gareth Edwards is to leave the ball with Mervyn Davies in the back row of the scrum, and to break flat across the field pretending to be carrying the ball. It is surprising how often the wing forward or opposite scrum-half are drawn offside by this move, thus giving a simple penalty. It happened in the fourth Test in South Africa in 1974 to bring the score level, 13–13.

Opposition Ball

On the opposition ball one should always attack and use every opportunity to give them poor possession. The eight-man shove is particularly effective here. With this shove the feet of each player should be pointed straight forward, giving maximum drive. The front row should bear down on the opposition, particularly the hooker, to make it difficult or impossible for him to strike. All players should be balanced and ready to lift and explode forward as the ball comes in to the scrum. They should concentrate on a specially tight bind and this grip with the arms coupled with the powerful drive from the legs combine to send the opposition back, or at least to make them either get bad ball or get ball on the retreat. This allows pressure to be put on the scrum-half, cuts out back row moves, and produces situations like the one in the fourth Test in Johannesburg in 1974 where Gareth Edwards pressurised Paul Baynel into giving a bad pass and Roger Uttley was on the ball in a flash and scored a try.

Timing is of the essence: too early a shove means coming back to the mark and losing the initiative: too late a shove means pushing when the ball has already been won. The folly of this was demonstrated in the Lions' second Test in 1971 where John Taylor and Peter Dixon were so committed to pushing that Sid Going was allowed to breech the initial defence, and set up a score, even though the All

Blacks were being pushed back in the scrum. The wing forwards must always be aware of the position of the ball, and if they are unsighted and the scrum is moving forward they should detach themselves and look after fringe defence. If the ball is won by the push they can help or set up attacks close to the scrum.

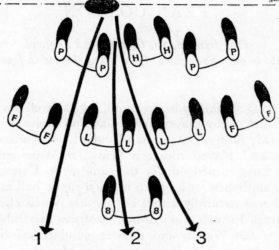

gain line

SCRUM CHANNELS

This diagram illustrates the three principal channels the ball should take for a successful heel. But correct feet positioning is also vital for good scrummaging.

Props should have their outside foot slightly in front of their inside foot, and should put their weight on the outside of the inside foot.

The outside feet of locks and flankers should also be in front of their inside feet or, in the case of the locks, can be in line.

No. 8's feet are in line, taking as much weight as possible. Some experienced props vary their feet positions and on the 1974 Lions tour Ian McLauchlan liked to have his right foot behind the hooker's left leg.

Kitted Out for Wigan

FRAN COTTON

Prop forward, 26, Coventry and England.
12 caps to end 1975 season. Lions 1974. Played in four Tests.

Considering my family background, I might well have been a professional rugby player, but I have no desire to play for money. My father, Dave, was a Rugby League international hooker, and played nineteen years for Warrington; my brother later turned out for the same club. I was born at Wigan, and when I was given my first rugby ball at the age of six I was naturally kitted out in the Wigan cherry and white strip. In such an environment it was inevitable that I should watch Wigan, and wish to emulate my Saturday afternoon heroes, Billy Boston and Brian McTigue, but once I started playing rugby seriously the call of Rugby League faded. Since winning international honours I have in fact turned down handsome offers from top League clubs, and my father agrees with my decision. We both think Rugby League is a dying game.

As a youngster I played rugby with boys in the neighbourhood at every spare moment, but my first chance to play on an organised basis came when I started at Newton-le-Willows Grammar School. It seemed natural to take up my father's position of hooker, but it was not long before I outgrew my props and decided to join their ranks. By the time I was sixteen my passion for rugby was such that I joined Newton-le-Willows Old Boys, playing for their colts team in the afternoons after playing for the school during the morning. I was lucky to come under an excellent coach, Don Gullick, who taught me an important principle about the game – that the ball should not be allowed to die. Backs

140

and forwards alike were encouraged to run and handle.

From Newton-le-Willows I was invited, at the age of 18, to join Liverpool on their Easter tour to Bath and Bristol. At school I had not gained any representative honours, but this trip gave me an insight into the rugby scene. The Liverpool team then had two England players, Tom Brophy and Ed Rudd, and at Bristol I played in front of an eight-thousand crowd – against such famous men as Dave Rollitt and Bill Redwood. Only a week before I had been in my local club side, with practically no one except an enthusiastic father watching. That first trip with Liverpool had a significant influence on me, as it made me realise I might become part of a truly big game.

My third first-class match was against Coventry, and after it I realised how much work I needed to do. That day I played against Phil Judd, the former England captain, and it left me so exhausted I had difficulty getting dressed after the game. Following this physical pounding I realised that strength and stamina were the prerequisites of a prop, and set about finding a remedy. I wrote to Malcolm Allison, then coach to Manchester City, and he kindly sent me some weight-training and road-running schedules, which I understand originally came from Jim Ryun, the American world mile record holder.

During my early days in senior rugby I met two coaches who fashioned my thinking about the game, John Burgess and Jim Greenwood. Burgess coached Lancashire and later took over the England team. I was selected for Lancashire in the same year he became county coach, 1967, and he started a revival which extended throughout rugby in the north of England. More than anyone else Burgess influenced my style and attitude to the game. In September 1970 I joined Loughborough Colleges as a student physical education teacher, and there came in touch with Greenwood, a Scot who had played with the 1955 Lions team in South Africa and another coach who thought progressively. He was a remarkable coach, who had detailed technical knowledge of every position on the field. Although he had played as No. 8 he taught me a lot about the front row. Burgess did not possess the same technical background as Greenwood, but had the great gift of being able to motivate players. During 1972 it was these two men who coached the first two English county combinations to beat an All Black team.

When I was first selected as loose head prop by Lancashire I was nineteen; I was too young, and was immediately dropped. It was at Loughborough that I had the chance of really learning my trade. Even at school I had an ambition to attend Loughborough but, partly because I had achieved so little sporting success, when the time came I decided to enter mine management instead. After a few years I decided that the future of the British Coal industry was limited, and I switched to a teaching career. I joined Loughborough, and found the Colleges had a number of outstanding players there – men like Steve Smith, John Gray, Lewis Dick, Clive Rees and Alan Cowman – all of whom except Gray gained full international honours.

My first major breakthrough came in November 1970 when I was selected for an England under-25 team against Fiji. England won the game and I was tipped as an immediate prospect for a full cap, but this hope was dimmed during a trial when I played loose head against Keith Fairbrother, then the current England tight head prop. It was then that I decided to move over to the tight head for Lancashire, though continuing to play on loose head for Loughborough. My ability to play on both sides of the front row has been a great help to me in gaining selection, especially on tours. At 6 ft 2 in I might be a shade too tall for the loose head position, as a smaller man who is just as strong has the advantage of better leverage.

During the 1970–71 season I was at the first three internationals as a travelling replacement, and watched the familiar sight of England showing promise but never fulfilling it. My proudest moment in rugby will be the day I played for England as tight head prop against Scotland –

and after two centenary matches I was selected for the Far East tour of autumn 1971.

This tour took place after the Lions' triumphs in New Zealand and inevitably England were compared with that team by the travelling Press. We were criticised for not adopting the Lions' style of overlap moves and brilliant counter-attacks, but this was not possible, as the basics – scrum, line-outs, ruck and maul – had to be perfected first. Burgess, the coach on that tour, endeavoured to achieve these basics as a way of preparing for the coming season. The players had been told it was all part of the build-up for the championship.

The England team overcame difficult climatic conditions to remain unbeaten, but the criticism lingered on and appeared to influence the national selectors. The next season only four members of the tour appeared in the first international. Burgess was also dropped, and it was no wonder after all this upheaval that England had their worst season ever, failing to win a single championship match.

I was one of those excluded from the international scene, but I was selected for England's 1972 tour of South Africa. It was generally thought that after such a season England would meet disaster touring the Republic for the first time, but instead we played seven matches without defeat and gained a historic victory over South Africa at Ellis Park, Johannesburg. Much of the credit for that success was due to the coach John Elders and England's new captain, John Pullin. Between them they built up such an excellent team spirit during the month on tour that the trip will remain a highlight of my career. I was satisfied with my personal performances, although I was not selected for the Test.

The next season was my best. The experience gained from playing with Loughborough and Lancashire improved my all-round game and I was recalled to the England team. Just as important, I led the North-West Counties team who beat the All Blacks in a game which demonstrated Burgess's tremendous grasp of tactics. Lancashire also won the county championship and at the end of the season I led the victorious England seven-a-side team in the world tournament held at Murrayfield to celebrate the Scottish R.U. centenary.

England were due to tour Argentina in 1973 but this was cancelled and a trip to Fiji and New Zealand was arranged instead. Many people questioned the wisdom of undertaking such a strenuous tour at the beginning of the season, but once again the combination of Elders and Pullin overcame early setbacks in provincial games and England went on to gain another historic victory in the Test against the All Blacks. As Sandy Sanders, the manager, said at the after-match function: 'England have won the crown jewel of rugby in beating the All Blacks at Eden Park.'

A year later I achieved the ambition of all rugby players, to be selected to tour with the Lions, and I played in all four Tests in South Africa. Now I can compare the forward play of the two famous Southern Hemisphere rugby countries and I would say the scrummaging is better in South Africa whereas the New Zealanders concentrate much more on the loose play and rucking. While the British and Irish forwards devote more attention to the maul which can be effectively controlled, the New Zealanders use this only as a last resort. They much prefer to ruck the ball on the ground. In approach the All Blacks are much more fierce and difficult to handle, but the Springbok tradition for scrummaging will ensure they revive quickly. South Africa's approach has always been to subdue forward and then penetrate; their lapse in 1974 will prove only temporary.

Rucking and Mauling

FRAN COTTON

The major factor in the success of the 1974 Lions in South Africa was the forwards' absolute dominance in the set-pieces. The reason I am so categorical about the importance of set-piece possession is that winning the ball going forward at the scrum and line-out affects so many other aspects of play. First, it means that the scrum-half can serve his backs unimpeded, while they are moving forward on to the ball, thus giving the three-quarter line extra pace. The opposing flank forwards are committed to pushing in the scrum, so relieving the pressure on your inside backs. The opposition three-quarters have to move back until the ball is released from the set-piece, which gives your own backs a vital extra yard to work their moves or get the ball out to the wing. All these factors have an important bearing on the result of a game, but I feel that there is one still more crucial – the psychological advantage of going forward.

While dominating in the set-pieces the 1974 Lions also won seventy per cent of the ruck and maul possession. Obviously one of the reasons for this overwhelming superiority was the superior technique of both forwards and backs. Above all else, each member of the team was running forward on to the ball.

Before I go into the techniques of rucking and mauling I should stress that these are phases of the game which result from a failure to score, and are methods of retaining or regaining possession after such a failure. It seems that some teams, like the All Blacks, have now made the setting up of a ruck or maul an aim in itself. This has led to a decline in three-quarter play and a stifling of attacking flair.

What is meant by a ruck or a maul, and what is meant by quality possession from these phases of play? A ruck is formed when the ball is on the ground, and one or more players from each team are on their feet and in physical contact, closing around the ball between them. A maul is formed by one or more players from each team, on their feet and in physical contact, closing around a player who is carrying the ball. A maul ends when the ball is on the ground, or the ball or the player carrying it emerges from the maul – and it also ends when a scrummage is ordered.

How does one decide when to ruck and when to maul? On the 1974 tour we had the simple tactic of trying to maul the ball when we were in possession and trying to knock the opposition to the ground and ruck the ball when *they* were in possession. It sounds easy, but it takes a great deal of skill to create a maul rather than a ruck. First it means that you have to take tackles on your own terms – in other words, you must remain on your feet after the tackle, and make the ball available to your colleagues. Support for the ball carrier must be instant: normally the person who has just passed the ball is in the best position for this. When the techniques are applied correctly the ball is under absolute control and can be given back to the scrum-half when he asks for it. Quality possession from a maul is when it is moving forward, and the ball is then given back to the scrum-half on request. If for some reason the maul becomes static then it is often best to roll off the side of the maul and drive the ball on.

When the opposition have the ball the main aim is to regain possession, and the most effective way to do this – if the opposing player does not kick the ball – is to knock him to the ground in the tackle, forcing him to release the ball. If possible the first person to the breakdown should pick the ball up and move it on, but failing that he should drive straight over the top of the ball. The players following in support should drive forward into the ruck in set-scrum formation, taking the opposition away from the ball and leaving it behind for the scrum-half. This is quality possession from a ruck.

It is interesting how different countries have developed the ruck rather than the maul and vice-versa. The South Africans tend to use the maul rather than the ruck, primarily because their hard grounds make the ball lively and difficult to control. In New Zealand the ruck has been developed and suits their regimented style of play, a style which is typified by one of their leading provincial coaches saying: 'I drop any forward who needs to think.'

In Britain the maul is being developed successfully, but yet more importance should be placed on it. We have a tremendous number of players who have sufficient innate ball-handling ability to master the art of mauling. Overall football skill has always been one of our main assets, so why not make use of it? During my days at Loughborough Colleges the coach, Jim Greenwood, developed the ruck rather than the maul; but he had very good reasons for doing so. He felt that the forwards at Loughborough did not have the required upper-body strength to compete with the more mature forwards they normally faced. I mention this to illustrate that a good coach must analyse the players he is coaching and develop a style of play to suit them.

Looking at the techniques involved, there seems to be greater uniformity on how the ruck should be formed. The most important point in winning good ruck ball is that you must be running forward on to the ball. To enable the forwards to do this it is the backs' responsibility to ensure that, after receiving the ball from the forwards, they cross the gain line either by running or by sensible kicking. If the ball received is not good ball there is little point in passing it on and making it worse. This is the time for sensible kicking, either to gain ground or to regain possession.

When tackled in possession and unable to stay on your feet you should set the ball up as favourably as possible for your own side. This means putting the ball behind you in such a way that your body protects it from the opposition but leaves it available to your team-mates. For instance, if the movement is going from left to right and you are tackled, as you are falling to the ground the ball should be placed behind you on the right hand side of your body.

The first support player – back or forward, depending on who is nearest the breakdown – should first think about picking the ball up and moving it on to the next player up in support. Failing this, he should try to take the opposition away from the ball by driving straight over the top of it. The two immediate supporting players should bind on to either side to form a front row. The first of these players should bind on the far side to stabilise and balance the ruck. Just as the front row of a set-scrum must be in a low shoving position it is equally important that the front row of a ruck should adopt exactly the same position, and try to pick up the opposition to take them away from the ball. Too many forwards think they have done their job by reaching the ruck; in fact their job has only just started.

These front three players are the platform on which the remaining forwards add momentum to the already formed ruck. Players should be driving forward parallel to the touchline. If the platform is in any way unbalanced the ruck invariably ends up in a morass of bodies with neither side winning the ball cleanly. Hence the importance of driving beyond the ball, so that if the ruck collapses the ball is left free.

When coaching rucking it should be drilled into players that they must work to get directly behind the ball, so that they will always be in the correct position should a ruck occur. Once the platform has been set up correctly and is moving forward the next two players should be concerned with adding impetus to the ruck by driving in directly behind. Again the principle is to go in hard and low but never to take your eye off the ball. There is nothing more infuriating than seeing the ball being kicked unknowingly through to the opposition.

When the ball is obviously going to be won from the ruck the last two forwards to arrive should not only add weight and drive – one on each side – but should also use their outside arms as hooks to tie in any 'seagulls' or 'fringers' from the opposition.

During a game a player will have many roles to play in the ruck, so as he approaches each ruck he must decide what his particular job will be. The good players are those who consistently make the right decision.

Now for mauling. The most important player in gaining possession from a maul is the ball carrier. Very often, when watching players whose ability I know, I can predict which side will win the maul as soon as I see the ball carrier. Any young player who wants to learn how to take a tackle on his own terms and set up a maul should watch Tony Neary. He is an expert in these close-quarter exchanges. Always on his feet, driving forward with the ball protected and available, he is the ideal example.

The ball must be held in two hands, on the far side of the tackler. When you adopt this position you automatically drop your shoulder into the would-be tackler, and are in a strong position to continue driving. Always strive to stay on your feet, so that the immediate supporter can rip the ball away from your grasp and get it as far away from the opposition as possible. Normally it is best to get the ball down close to the ground so that no stray arms prevent you from delivering it back cleanly.

Now the ball has been secured, it is up to the rest of the support to take the opposition away from the ball carrier by driving past him. Again it is important to *think* when approaching any maul and decide at which position you should enter. If the maul becomes unbalanced – because more players are on one side than the other – it will rotate and finish up in a tangle of arms and legs on the ground.

In discussing the techniques of ruck and maul I have assumed that support for the ball carrier has been there. Obviously the winning of a ruck and maul also depends upon force of numbers. If one player is struggling against three it doesn't matter how good his technique may be: his team is unlikely to win the ball. Speed and concentration are the key words in ensuring that your players get to the break-down faster and in greater numbers than the opposition. Forwards have to be told to shove and run and jump and run, the backs tackle and run and pass and support.

What should a team do if they are losing the rucks or mauls? Usually the first five or six players to the breakdown will be unable to decide whether they will win it or lose it. The vital players are the last forward to arrive and the scrum-half. One should mark the blind side and one the open side. Opinion varies as to who does which, but I think that the scrum-half is better suited to taking the blind side while the forward takes the open side. The short side is the dangerous attacking area and scrum-halves are better equipped to deal with the probes of their opposite number than a prop or hooker.

The scrum-half, incidentally, is never more important than in ruck and maul situations. If he is getting the ball cleanly and when he wants he is in the ideal position to decide how to continue the attack, either by passing, kicking or breaking himself.

In theory, if players were skilful enough the game should never stop except after a try has been scored. One of the major reasons for frequent breakdowns, apart from lack of skill, is the lack of total game appreciation – the ability to make the right decision according to the state of the play. This involves assessing the best use to which each player can put himself – for instance, whether he should commit himself to being tackled so as to form a ruck or maul. Sometimes the right decision may be to stop a yard short in order to retain possession, other times it may be better to drive the ball on. On other occasions mauls are formed when the ball carrier could have sent a team-mate crashing on with the ball towards his opponents' line. The one certainty is that the complete team is one of fifteen thinking players.

TRAINING

How do you start on the road to becoming a British Lion?

I have asked myself this question many times and I always give myself the same answer – dedication. This means setting the highest standards of physical fitness and never being disheartened when things go wrong. A failure can be better than a fortuitous success, as only after failure does one closely examine how one can improve. As I look back on my early training days the light of experience tells me I wasted much of my time, and I am sure that this applies to many other players. My days at Loughborough made me realise that the value of a training session should not be judged on time but on intensity.

A training programme which has proved worthwhile for me includes 'Fartlek', a Scandinavian idea starting with a series of short bursts, then jogging and subsequently fast running to build up speed and stamina. My training programme follows.

Mid-June	Three times a week:	ROAD RUN – 3–4 miles, trying to improve time taken.
		GENERAL WEIGHTS AND EXERCISES.
July	Three times a week:	FARTLEK – starting time 20 mins. building up to 45 mins. Intensity of session always chief aim.
		WEIGHTS – 3 exercises:
		1. Dead Lift
		2. Squat
		3. Bench Press.
August	Once a week:	FARTLEK – 45 minutes.
	Twice a week:	INTERVAL TRAINING – 8 ×220 yds.
		WEIGHTS – as before.
		CLUB TRAINING
September *October* *November*	Twice a week	INTERVALS – 6 ×440 yds. 8 ×330 yds. 10 ×220 yds.
	Once a week	HILL SPRINTS
		WEIGHTS – as before.
		CLUB TRAINING
Rest of *season*	One	STAMINA SESSION
	One	WEIGHTS SESSION
	Two	SPRINTS SESSIONS
		CLUB TRAINING

Triple Crown Baby

FERGUS SLATTERY

Flanker, 26, Blackrock and Ireland.
25 caps to end 1975 season. Lions 1971–74. Four Tests.

As a rugby player my birthday has a special personal significance. My birth, on Saturday morning, 12 February 1949, caused both apprehension and amazement for our family doctor. The bold doctor's thoughts lay more with happy events in Belfast than those in Dublin. His apprehension was caused by my forthcoming birth, because any hold-up would delay his departure to Belfast (Ravenhill, to be precise). That day Ireland were playing their vital Triple Crown game in a bid to retain the Crown they had won the previous year. My arrival was fortunately on schedule, but after the weigh-in the doctor was amazed to find that the scales tipped 12 lbs. However, this did not deter him departing with haste for Ravenhill, where he saw Ireland win their second Triple Crown. It was also Ireland's last – a fact that has stuck in the back of my mind.

After many years spent in Malaya with my family I took my place in the schoolboy section at Lansdowne Road at the age of nine, and thereafter watched Ireland play many games in what was undoubtedly a difficult era in Irish football.

There seemed to be few outstanding victories but the success against the 1958 Wallabies and great 1959 French team captivated my imagination. The Irish have a national trait of knocking their own, especially in rugby, without considering the difficulties. Rugby is only the fourth most popular grass game behind Gaelic Football, hurling and soccer. Rugby never prospered in Ireland like other coun-

153

tries due to the ban, recently lifted, by the Gaelic Athletic Association which prevented their members taking part in what were described as garrison games (those played by British soldiers). Now the ban has been lifted I think rugby will grow considerably, but this will not be seen until the '80s when more people from the rural areas start playing.

Historically, rugby in Ireland has been a city game played in Dublin, Limerick, Belfast, Cork and Galway, but non-existent in the villages. I think the basis for the strength of any sport is that it must be played in the villages. An important factor favouring rugby is that it is one game where the Irish have achieved some sort of parity on an international level. Gaelic football and hurling are confined to Ireland, and our soccer has not been able to keep up with the standards in Europe.

I first played rugby at Presentation College, Glasthule, in a variety of positions ranging from full-back to prop forward. Later I was to attend Blackrock College, one of the great rugby nurseries in Ireland. It was here that I first learned of the discipline and rigorous training which rugby football demanded, and, most important of all, coaching. I played for the junior school side in 1964, a team which remained un-defeated for the entire season and which captured the junior Schools Cup.

The following year, ironically, proved to be one of the most valuable in my rugby career. I was left in limbo, being too old for the junior side and not good enough for the senior side. It was during this year that I recognised and adopted a number of fundamental principles which I thought were necessary to get into the school's senior team. I realised that skill and talent would never be sufficient for any player to achieve his ultimate goal. I decided that to progress I would have to try harder than everyone else, both on the pitch and more especially in training. I set goals in my train-ing and competed against my colleagues whenever I could. During our afternoon recreation period we often trained with unopposed rugby. This exercise was primarily to improve on second phase possession. Here I set myself the task of getting to the breakdown first, be it from the set-piece, ruck or maul. To succeed in my goal I had to run flat out from the set-piece to the breakdown, disengage from the maul and sprint across to the wing, often overtaking a couple of forwards on the way. This helped to improve my speed, stamina, strength, and – most important of all – the ability to read where and when the breakdown would occur.

In the evenings we ran a circuit of approximately two miles on the roads, usually splitting up into three or four groups. In this I was unable to outrun one particular player and I therefore decided to run two circuits in order to make up for this failing. Introducing this competitive instinct made training far more enjoyable, and, when at last I succeeded in getting into the school's senior team, all the more worthwhile.

I also came to see the weaknesses in my basic skills, such as running, handling, passing, tackling and kicking. From then on I always used the free moments – those two to three minutes when we were assembling for training – to work on any particular weakness in my game. In using just a few minutes every day I soon learned to kick effectively with both feet, to pass as well to the right as I did to the left, and so on. By the time I left school I had begun thinking about my game, back row play, and was prepared to work hard to bring about these necessary improvements. I was then 17 and joined Blackrock College R.F.C. After three months of rugby with the junior teams I was selected to play for the first XV, and retained my position for the remainder of the season. It was during this season that I learned another lesson – this time a very bitter one.

Playing for a club selected side I received a bad tear to the lateral ligaments of the right knee. I played for the rest of the season, with a heavily bandaged knee, regardless of the discomfort which the injury caused, but I did incalculable damage when I really needed six to eight weeks' rest. The knee also had to contend with the rigours of soccer, as in addition to rugby I was playing for a local club side at right-back. Often I was playing as many as three matches in a weekend and training with the rugby side and soccer sides, too, and I paid for it the following season. I had to give up soccer, and, after four or five weeks, rugby too. So for one season I sat on the side-lines, all because I had not given an injury the proper chance to heal. Even since I have had the greatest respect for even the smallest injuries, and have learned some effective ways to treat common injuries from medical friends.

In 1969 I decided to play with University College, Dublin, where I had been studying since I left school. It was here that I began to train harder than ever before. The environment was perfect, and the competition fierce amid an atmosphere of friendship and goodwill, and this instilled a rare spirit into the players and teams at the university.

This spirit which prevailed has in itself made rugby worth playing. I played alongside many good players including Barry Bresnihan, Tom Grace, Tony Ensor, Seamus Deering, Kevin Mays and Con Feighery, all of whom have worn the green jersey of Ireland. The environment of university rugby is the best there is: an exploring ground for rugby, with supreme effort and eagerness to improve, all of which are difficult to parallel elsewhere. In the three years I played at U.C.D. discipline and confidence were added to my game, much of it due to the way the players worked towards helping each other's games.

The 1971 Lions tour of Australia and New Zealand was of course a tremendous experience, a chance to learn from the other players, and more especially from Carwyn James. It was only the second time since leaving school that I came under a coach. Ronnie Dawson had been the Irish national team coach since 1969, and he did much to mould my attitudes towards the game both on and off the field.

Carwyn James taught me many of the refinements of the game and he even managed to dispel some of those bad habits which one so easily acquires. He taught me such simple things as carrying the ball with both hands while running rather than tucking it half way up your jersey. He drilled the lesson home of picking up the loose ball off the ground rather than kicking it away upfield – simple things, but they all add up.

I was also given the opportunity to examine the merits and demerits of our own type of football compared with the New Zealand brand. It is probably stating the obvious when I say that I found the New Zealand game hard and uncompromising, with the major emphasis on their forwards. This has paid dividends for a good many years, but the tide has changed and they fell behind in the arts of scrummaging compared to British and Irish forwards. It did not take them long to learn, as seen during their unbeaten short tour of Ireland, Wales and England in 1974.

So to the 1974 tour of South Africa, and that unbeaten record over twenty-two matches. It would have been twenty-two wins if I had been awarded a try in the closing minutes of the final Rest match. So much has been written and said about this 'try' that I welcome the opportunity to have my say for the first time.

Chris Ralston took a clean catch in the line-out and the ball seemed to move slowly across to the left wing until J. P. R. Williams joined in. I had noticed the angle of his approach and went outside to the left of him. Williams was checked near the posts and I called for the ball, but had to stop to take it. From almost a standing position I checked inside to the right towards the posts off my left foot. Piet Cronje was almost standing on the line but I did not have the time or flexibility to change as one would have wanted. There was only a space of a few yards, and I had to go into Cronje and hit him with my shoulder. Unfortunately my momentum was not strong enough. He fell back onto his backside and I fell into him with the ball in my hands. I then pulled the ball down my chest between his and my legs to ground the ball, lying half on top of him. As I was about to ground the ball I remember Paul Bayvel, South Africa's scrum-half, screaming: 'He hasn't touched it. No try, no try. He hasn't touched it.'

Not for a second did I ever consider I had not scored a fair try. I never heard the referee – Max Baise – blow the whistle, and it was only from the reaction of those around me that I knew the try had not been given. Cronje got up on his feet and said: 'I am sorry about that.' Baise was unfortunately behind Cronje's back and not in a good position to judge whether I had scored a fair try or not.

The vast majority of referees' decisions are right, and you must abide by them even if they are wrong. You must also realise that, in the modern game, television can detect what a referee can not see. It is very easy to criticise afterwards, but if one wants to put the microscope to anything one can always find fault.

After the try was disallowed I was not as upset as some of the other players around me because I still felt we would score. When a five-yard scrum was awarded following the dispute I became more determined to get a try. I felt we were far stronger than them and if we really turned it on we would score the points.

The scrum ball was won and J. J. Williams tried to make the line, but was caught and a maul followed. It was hardly set up when the whistle went – a premature decision. Irrespective of whether Gareth Edwards had got the ball, I am certain we would have scored given another minute. The side had the character to produce the goods when the pressure was really on. Mervyn Davies and Roger Uttley were in there to get the ball, and it was coming back for another movement, and Gareth might well have scored. He is an exceptionally strong physical player and it is difficult to stop him near the line. Anyway, it is wrong for players to come off the field and consider one disputed decision lost them the game. Rugby is far bigger than that. Also, good teams make their own luck.

Unfortunately the Lions did not have the right mental attitude for that last Test match. After the final provincial game the Tuesday before, it would have been better if the selected team and reserves had gone out of Johannesburg and prepared for one final mighty effort. Instead we did not do ourselves justice at Ellis Park. Rugby is played over 80 minutes and you can't always get away with a supreme effort in the final few minutes. We had survived with late revivals against both Orange Free State and Natal, but you can't go on surviving like that.

The Lions' ability to revive late had been seen in the last major provincial game, against Natal in Durban the previous Saturday. Although the series was then won we were defending an unbeaten record. Ten minutes from the end against Natal I realised we had lost our edge. Players had started to think about going home, and once this happens it is very difficult to get them to concentrate on the game ahead. In Durban eight minutes from the end we were under a frightening amount of pressure, and yet the team still had the conviction to pull back and score many points during the last minutes – including injury time.

Motivation is the key factor in producing a winning team. Everyone must be built up on the same plane before they go out on the field. Whatever game you play where the opposition is about equal strength no one side can dominate from start to finish. If you succeed for twenty minutes you cannot hope to keep that up for the remaining sixty. In an individual or team game performances can be shown in a graph – with highs and lows. You reach a high, level out, and then drop. When you drop it must be controlled, and your play consolidated, to stave off the impending trough.

Once the opposition senses any slackness they become encouraged and move up to their high as you are going down. Consequently at that stage they are going to pick up points. Even a commanding position can quickly be lost. If you don't regain it very quickly you can find yourself in a position of losing a game due to an inability to control that psychological factor which affects everyone's performance.

In an individual game you are working for yourself,

whereas in a team game you have ten or fourteen others and
it's a matter of co-ordinating those players so they have the
same train of thought. Players must realise before they go out
on the field that they will reach these sort of situations. You
may start off a game and be beaten for twenty minutes, but
you have go to pull together and get back on top.

The captain is a man with two responsibilities, motivation
and direction. Motivation must begin before the game starts
but direction depends on the actual flow of play and how
that is assessed. Then you have either to get into the game or
hold it. When working together as a team it is vital to utilise
all resources.

There is no golden formula for captaincy. John Dawes and
Willie John McBride were both highly successful, but very
different in their approach. Both commanded respect from
their players both on and off the field, as they were both outstanding players who made a major individual contribution
to the team. On a long tour the activities of a captain off the
field are an important factor. In terms of quality of leadership John Dawes was a fine administrator who knew the
whys and why nots. The great quality of McBride will
always be his simplicity. There is no player in this world that
Willie could not communicate with under any situation or
circumstance. It would not matter if he was dealing with an
A team player.

Having toured both major Southern Hemisphere countries, I would say the New Zealand game is far more physical.
They use more of the boot on the deck, and some of the teams
we played overdid it. A few players took pleasure out of this
and it's a great pity to see the game drop to those depths. I
don't agree with the New Zealand idea of getting a man off
the ball. You can heel a man off, but I totally disagree with
kicking him. I accept it happens everywhere – but slightly
more in New Zealand. Munster rugby in Ireland has always
been very fierce, and in some club sides you come up against
the same mentality found in New Zealand. Some of the
Welsh club sides are tough – and mean; but fortunately this

approach is seldom seen in the five-countries championship.

During a major tour of New Zealand you play against stronger provincial teams than in South Africa, where there are a number of mediocre provinces. Even the weaker sides in New Zealand are tough and rugged. South Africa is a vast country and this adds to the problems of competitive rugby at provincial level.

On every major tour you always come across one or two sides who will set out to beat the visitors by bruising play. In 1971 the New Zealand team which really went out to beat us in a totally physical game was Canterbury. One or two other sides also concentrated on this approach, like Taranaki and Hawkes Bay.

Six or seven Canterbury players were unnecessarily physical. I was concussed after about eight or nine minutes and remained in that condition until about ten minutes into the second half. I remember asking Peter Dixon after twenty minutes where we were, and he had to tell me I was playing against Canterbury. It didn't mean anything to me at the time and about five minutes into the second half I said: 'Peter, where are we?' He looked at me, completely taken aback, but he couldn't answer because he didn't know himself. Instead he told me to clear off. I only realised where I was in the final quarter of the game.

Two of my teeth were broken, but fortunately they were saved by a former All Black, Keith Nelson, a dentist in Auckland. I remember the incident that did the damage very well. It was following a line-out on our 25; we won the ball when I was smashed by a front row forward. I wasn't even looking at him.

The difference between the two Lions teams I toured with was in their respective distribution of strengths. The 1971 side had a better all-round back division, while the one in South Africa had tremendous forward power. Both had the right attitude, the right discipline, were well coached, and played ten-man rugby when the conditions or situation dictated. Overall I think the thirty players who went to

South Africa were better than those who went to New Zealand. In Test situations the '74 team could always gain possession.

Another difference – one of the important ones – between the tours was that in 1974 we were under pressure throughout, defending an unbeaten record. In contrast the 1971 side were beaten in Australia and then in the second Test about the middle of the tour. After that the team took on a new lease of life. When you are unbeaten you can only go on winning. It creates a psychological problem which the 1974 team had until the end of the tour. But both parties have established a foundation for the future of Lions' tours, which is important.

South Africa's weakness was not that they lacked international competition, nor that they had lost so many good players, but that they could not put together the right combination of players. Instead of developing their own game they were concerned with 'taming the Lions'. Their selectors did not appear to know the type of players they needed to cope with the Lions' forward strength. They also made some fundamental mistakes, like playing a hooker with only a few months' experience and a scrum-half who was a No. 8 the previous season. In the third Test they dropped their own John Williams (not to be confused with J. P. R. or J. J.), yet he was their best line-out jumper.

The Pivot Five

FERGUS SLATTERY

In the past, the Southern Hemisphere has dominated the rugby scene, and tended to go for big, chunky back row forwards. New Zealand play very much to their back row, using them to bring the ball back to the forwards. The South Africans have had a similar approach to the game. This used to pay dividends, but today the game has changed – and so have the responsibilities placed on the back row.

Obviously the strength of your tight forwards determines the leeway you can give to size and height among the back row forwards. It is essential to have tall men, particularly in the line-out because you cannot rely on the No. 8 alone. At the same time it is not essential to have three tall back row forwards. In 1971 Peter Dixon, in three Tests and Derek Quinnell, once, played at No. 6. Roger Uttley played there in all four in 1974.

The major difference between the two tours was the change in the line-out laws in 1973. Because of the new rules regarding spacing and compression the strategy we adopted in 1971 was far more difficult to apply in 1974. For instance, it was impossible to contest openly in the line-out with the same physical vigour as before.

I don't agree with the concept of 'open' and 'blind'. The fastest forward should play at the end of the line-out, but not on a particular side of the scrum. The idea of putting a big flank forward always on the loose head is dangerous, because this is the area frequently used by the scrum-half to attack. Tony Neary and myself are very similar in most aspects of our game, and we played only once together – against Natal. We might have suffered from lack of height at the end of the line-out, but a tall No. 8 and two flankers over 6 ft should be able to cope with the line-out situation.

It is important in the modern game that the back row unit and half-backs work together and become the pivot five. This provides the perfect link-up with all the backs and produces the right association to cope with the various aspects of play.

Fortunately, in the British Isles, recent times have brought about a vast improvement in these relationships. The backs now place a greater faith and reliance on the supporting and attacking attributes of the back row. This is not confined to the supporting and attacking roles, but includes the securing and controlling of possession. Quite often a back is checked or smothered by a half-tackle, and is immediately involved in a grapple for possession. It is in the best interest of the back row and the player who has been checked that they both work in unison in order to secure immediate possession. The back caught in a half-tackle should hold his ground, stay on his feet, and turn inwards with his back to his opponent. He could, alternatively, drive forward, but this tends to envelop the player in the opposing players, thus losing or nullifying possession.

If the player has immediate support then the drive is on, but otherwise he should secure his position and set up the platform for the flank forward. The checked player has now given some protection to the ball, and has made it visible to his supporting flanker, who must now secure the ball and add to the wall set up by the back player. The next supporting player will bind in on the flank, thus forming a front line, and so on until a full maul is formed. The one major problem the flanker faces is how to secure the ball, since as often as not two or three unwanted arms or hands will have encroached around it.

The Chinese proverb, 'many hands make light work,' could not be further from the truth in the context of setting up a maul. Too many players grappling for the ball inevitably end up in a tug of war, with a negative result.

164

The tidying-up role of a back row forward is another important area of his game, because he secures possession from the uncontrolled loose ball. Dropped passes, and the stray balls from the set-scrums and line-outs, are the principal areas which require tidying up. Far too little is seen of players killing the loose ball on the ground, either through laziness, unwillingness or lack of emphasis by team coaches. If a player goes about it the right way, the chances of injury are no less or no more than in any other part of the game.

Here the positive approach is essential. The technique is fairly simple (although constant practice is needed if the basics are to be perfected). When falling try to smother the ball with both hands, your arms drawing it in close to your body. The speed and line of your approach must be judged accordingly. Remember that you are killing the ball with your back to the opposition.

During our training schedules on the Lions tour in New Zealand '71 Carwyn James always took time to practise the basics both for individuals and in unit play. A lot of time was given to controlling the 'sloppy' ball on the ground. As individuals we practised running into the rolling ball, falling on it and in the one movement rolling back on to our feet. Sometimes Carwyn took the two packs aside, with one pack defending and the second acting as aggressors. Carwyn stood between the two packs with the ball, releasing it in any direction. The defending pack had to get there first with one man falling and getting back on to his feet with the ball, and the remainder setting up the maul. These two exercises were done in almost every training session, reaping many dividends by the end of the tour.

One last word on that sloppy ball on the deck. The earlier the ball is killed the easier it is. Hesitancy will inevitably lose you ground – often half the length of the field. A loose ball from the set-pieces if left unattended by the back row, will bring pressure on the half-backs, often making their job more awkward; therefore *kill that loose ball at source* – make sure you come up if you can.

It is often said possession is nine-tenths of the law, and therefore an opportunity to regain possession must be seized wholeheartedly. These opportunities present themselves when a player is either caught or tackled in possession. If a player is caught it is important that he is turned away from his own support, and that his arms are held back. This will give the ball some exposure to your support players. Once again, it is important that the lead players avoid grappling for the ball as previously discussed.

I have assumed in these illustrations that the players are of equal parity, strength and size-wise. I would not have expected Colin Meads to look for support if he had caught a nine-stone scrum-half. When a player is tackled into the ground, the tackler has the advantage, having a bind on his opponent, and this advantage must be fully utilised if possession is to be regained. As soon as you have tackled the player you must quickly get back on your feet and advance over the player using either your hands or feet to release the ball, the latter being the more effective. You should not have taken possession (if only in theory) from your opponent.

The legislative changes, coupled with the general progression of the game through coaching, brought about a rapid development and change of emphasis in back-row play during the past decade. The role of the back-row forward in Ireland, Wales, England and Scotland, has changed dramatically. The back row forward has always been essentially a middleman, but recent law alterations have broadened his spectrum, and given him an even greater role in the game.

The game has always been conducive to back row forwards, because as middlemen they have been involved irrespective of the pattern of the game or the prevailing conditions. The back row community were traditionally marauders, and each back row player's status was often determined by the number of semi-precious half-back skins he had hanging up at the end of the season.

The game in the British Isles has only recently developed to the standards set by the New Zealanders and South Africans, and has in the past few years caught up and indeed overtaken them in many aspects. Considerable emphasis was placed on the attacking role down under.

Despite this emphasis, however, the basics remain the same. Broadly these may be categorised into defence, retention and tidying of possession. The application of the latter can be one of the most effective weapons in a back row armoury. Pressure may be applied in a number of ways, but the end result must be the same. It is the ability to limit your opponents' time and options, and therefore determining the course of play to a degree.

Pressure can be effectively put on the halves from the line-outs, rucks and maul, and to a lesser extent the set-scrum. One of the most effective ways of unbalancing a side is to split the half-back combination. This can dislodge the rhythm and confident approach of a three-quarter line. Upsetting the half-back is simply getting in between the scrum-half and out-half, and effectively reducing their opportunities of linking up.

The line-out provides an excellent pivot for the tail-end flanker, especially where the ball is thrown short to the second or third jumper. It is imperative that the flanker leaves the line-out at the earliest possible moment, and this requires judgment and concentration. The flanker must assess during the flight of the throw-in whether or not the jumper is tapping or catching, and whether he is under pressure from his opposite number.

Basically, he must try to assess the quality of the possession to be. If the ball is tapped back the flanker should be off the end of the line as the ball is about to be tapped. This will ensure that he has moved five or six yards before even the scrum-half has got possession of the ball. The speed of the scrum-half's adjusting and passing of the ball is pitted against the speed of the flanker and often as not it is very close. Thus the scrum-half may have to battle on his own ground, and here the hooker should be pressurising from the front of the line-out, thus snookering the half-back.

Ruck and maul situations call upon judgment and communication, with possibly a greater risk of being off-side. The flanker invariably covers the open side of the ruck-maul while the scrum-half takes the narrow side. Communication with another forward is imperative, because, if one can clearly determine that the opposition have secured possession, the flanker should draw one of his colleagues out of the ruck or maul to defend about two or three yards to the side. This enables the flanker to move further out and get closer to the out-half. This operation relies on communication and speed to react, and is also an effective way of pressurising and often splitting half-backs.

There are other ways of applying pressure on the half-back, although I doubt very much if they are all listed in the Queensbury rules. These include such devices as talking to the opposite half, and one of the great exponents of this was Noel Murphy, the Irish flank forward. He was noted as having developed this to an art. Talking at the half-backs distracts, annoys and quite often upsets players' concentration, and increases their awareness that there are back row forwards around.

A player who has the happy knack of being in the right place at the right time is automatically a good support player. It is the ability to read a situation before it arises, allied with a firm belief in the concept of support itself. This should provide a player with the motivation to keep up with the front runners for eighty minutes. This faith or belief in support is the firm realisation that sooner or later it will turn up trumps.

Take the young child who knows that the cookies are in the jar on the top shelf. He will need little motivation to get up there, but if the jar is concealed and the quantity is unknown his reactions may be very different.

In the same way a rugby player has got to be convinced that support will bring its results. Constant support should be instinctive, as it is in France and the two South Sea Islands, Fiji and Tonga. These rugby races have a flair for support – it seems to come so easily to them, almost effortlessly, while the rest of us labour and appear mechanical.

The French particularly amaze me. I remember one game in 1972. Due to the cancellations of the Scotland and Wales games, France played a second fixture against Ireland at Lansdowne Road. It was in this game that the Frenchmen scored two superb tries, both as a consequence of good support. Yet in the match they were under a great deal of pressure and, in fact, lost heavily. Despite this, on two occasions, one from a line-out and the second a scrum, they were able to score two wonderful tries and from inside their own half. The first came from a bad tap from the end of our line. Skrela picked up the loose ball, slipped it to Esteve, who in turn moved it on until finally Bertranne scored in the corner. There was nothing the Irish team could do to stop it, the support was so quick and in such depth that Tom Kiernan and Barry McGann were left with so many options it did not really matter whom they tackled. The second French try was just as quick and effective, this time from a 'wheel' in the scrum. Once again the loose ball was gathered and the support was like lightning. The wonderful thing about these two tries was the way a team could react to a given situation despite the fact that their morale could not have been mountain high. *The instinct was there.*

Support players should indicate positively to the ball carrier, by shouting 'left Jeff', or 'inside Eric'. Indicate where you are, and not just shout out, 'Pass Jeff', etc., or the like. After all, the player may be under pressure, and there may be two or three others shouting for the one ball. One further point: it is always a bonus when linking to take the ball on the burst.

There are limitless opportunities for the back row to attack from broken play. The scrum-half's half break off the ruck-mauls and set-pieces, the inside pass from the fly-half, the pass off the 'Rangi' or midfield switch, inside or outside passes from the full-back and wings. More often than not the ball the back row receives from these instances makes him an extra man, so his distribution is tantamount to success. I was involved in two separate incidents in the second Test on the '74 Lions tour of South Africa where my distribution made a situation.

The first move involved a midfield thrust by J. P. R. Williams. I took the ball on his outside with room to move in, plus support from a centre and wing. I was confronted on my inside by wing Chris Pope, who was coming across field to the full-back, who was on the outside. I decided to go between the two and managed to slip inside the full-back but was felled short of the line by Pope. My pass to our supporting centre did not find him and a try was lost. I had gambled and should have given the ball to the centre. He would then have drawn the full-back, fed the wing who should have made the corner. Even if cut off by Pope, he would have been able to pass back inside for a try. The second incident followed minutes later. This time I made amends by taking a loose ball off the back of a ruck, breaking open and giving a switch pass back inside to Phil Bennett who danced his way over the line for a try.

A final note: the back row should always know what their back line is up to, whether the kick is going to the box, to the post, diagonally across field, whether the movement is going left/right, or if there is a switch in midfield. Therefore communication is essential.

Let me make a few simple points about running with the ball. Carry the ball always in both hands, unless you are employing the hand-off. Never hit or drive into an opponent with the shoulder side the ball is being carried. Try and keep the ball as free as you can, so that it can be distributed. If you are, or know you are about to be, tackled and you have not found your support, try and ride the tackle keeping the ball free. This gives you a couple of extra seconds to distribute the ball.

The eight-man scrum is an accepted part of rugby in these

islands and has been established by recent overseas tours to New Zealand and South Africa. The back row have in the past been poor neighbours for the tight forwards and still are in the Southern Hemisphere in relation to the set-scrum. New Zealand and South Africa have for a long time advocated big back row forwards. This is all very well, but in the context of back row defence and the scrum it has not worked out well. The back rows on the 1972–73 All Blacks tour to the British Isles and those used by South Africa during the '74 Lions tour nearly all broke early from the scrum leaving only six forwards to pack against eight. Against eight men this left a deficit on their scrummaging accounts. Flank forwards can do two jobs, scrum and defend off the set-piece. Initially the opposition scrum will be a seven-man effort when the hooker is striking, and ultimately an eight-man drive. Therefore flank forwards have to learn to stay down and push until that ball is out.

If one accepts that the loose head side flank takes the first man in defence, the No. 8 the second man on that side, and that the scrum-half takes the first man on the tight head side with the right flank taking the second, then the following may make sense. In a defensive position the loose head flank is the one under most pressure as he takes the first man around, who is inevitably the scrum-half. While at University College, Dublin, I developed a simple defensive technique to cope with this situation. I always packed on the loose head, with my head half in the tunnel so that I could see the opposition scrum-half putting the ball into the scrum. Once he had the ball in his hands for the 'put-in', I never lost sight of it until right up to the moment he picked it up at the base of the scrum. This in no way affected my scrummaging nor any contribution to the set-scrum. It takes some time to perfect and is essential not to lose visual contact, even if the scrum is untidy.

Sometimes you lose sight of the ball and then it is important to come off the side of the scrum. If you can keep an eye on the ball and track it to the base of the scrum, then you can judge by watching the half-back's hands when he is about to pick it up. This enables you to move off the scrum in good time to cope with any 'starry-eyed' scrum-half. It is also important that when you come off the scrum you break at a forty-five degree angle as this will enable you to cover a scrum-half with fast heels. If you plunge straight forward a quick heel and a good pick up by the half-back may leave you in no man's land.

The right side flank or tight head is under far less pressure except when there is a strike against the head, and in that instance he is responsible for the first man on his side and the No. 8 the second. When defending, and the opposing scrum half breaks laterally, the flanker should stay with him all the way even if the scrum-half intimates a switch back inside with a three-quarter. The man taking the switch pass is marked by the No. 8. The No. 8 when breaking from the scrum in defence tends to rely on anticipation, but the scrum-half calling 'lost' and then 'break' makes his exit far more easily.

Defence – ruck and maul

The normal practice when forming rucks or mauls is to leave the last man out. The defence is then organised between him and the scrum-half. The simplest criterion is to let the scrum-half take the blind side and the last man takes the open side. This should work effectively, and is certainly the simplest method.

These moves help to bring variety to the game and also cross the tackle (or advantage) line.

Back row attacks are generally more difficult to execute than those in the three-quarter line, because you are working in a more confined space, and with less time. Therefore practice is essential. This was brought home to me in university where we adopted three standard ploys over as many years. Each back row forward was involved in a major way in at least one of the three. It took months of effort to perfect these, but we achieved considerable success.

Before back row moves can be contemplated there must be a platform – solid scrum to win good ball. Unless this is achieved you can discount back row moves – except perhaps No. 8 picking up, or the scrum half breaking and moving the ball back inside to the flanks. Back row moves are normally attempted within 25 yards of the opponent's line – why I don't know. There must be a reason, or the circumstances must present themselves, before one attempts a ploy and time and place must be used to best effect. The more time and effort given, the greater the relationship between the players involved, the more satisfactory the results. Below I set out a few ploys which have worked effectively and gained the desired result.

This first move involves only one flank forward, the one who packs down behind the loose head prop; timing is of the utmost importance. The flank breaks off the scrum and runs flat into the narrow side, timing his break with the put-in. The scrum-half passes directly to the flank who is lying up flat in the stand-off position. Ideally, if the move is executed and the channel in the scrum is clean, the flanker is still moving while the scrum-half passes. The fly-half moves into the open side, drawing his opposite number. This gives the flanker an open space to run into and from here he either draws the opposing blind side wing and feeds to his own wing, or he runs hard inside the opposing wing, eventually passing to a support player. Such a move surprises the opposing flank forward, as the attacking flanker has come from the far side of the scrum and some five to eight yards' ground should have been gained.

Let me make a few final points: it is important that the No. 8 channels the ball quickly over to the right side and releases immediately for the scrum-half to move the ball out. At University College, Dublin, we practised this move dili-gently and the results were rewarding. We developed a second move to cope with a slow or badly channelled ball, because with a delay the opposing flank can cancel out the original move. So the variation gives a gap for the scrum-half to exploit with the support of the outside flank and wing.

In the 1970 Leinster Cup Final, University College, Dublin, played Terenure College for the trophy. After twenty minutes of the game Tommy Doyle (Terenure) left the field with a cut eye. Shortly afterwards U.C.D. were awarded a scrum on their own ten-yard line and about fifteen yards from the touchline. Now as their back row were reduced to two we tried this ploy. Our fly-half drew his man to the open side, and I received the scrum-half's pass on the narrow side and went through the gap. Before being tackled by the full-back I had transferred to our right wing, Tom Grace, who scored in the corner.

I have great faith in the universal ploy of the No. 8 picking up and moving into the right side with support from the flank on the inside or outside. Done positively this move is very effective but it is important that the flank forward has a sound relationship with the No. 8. Another ploy, although more difficult, works well. This move is well known to New Zealanders and involves the No. 8 moving across and packing between the left flank and the lock and the right side flank moving into the No. 8 spot. The ball is channelled to the No. 8 who picks and turns into the opposing scrum-half, driving a few yards and slipping to the flank who has come from the No. 8 position. This must be done quickly in order to set the flank clear.

Carwyn James introduced another variation during the course of the 1971 Lions tour in New Zealand. The right side flank broke off the scrum and took the scrum-half's pass. He then drove into the defending flank as close to the side of the scrum as possible, causing a bottle-neck for the opposite flank and No. 8. This move was closely supported by the No. 8, whose job was to snatch the ball off the flank's hip on impact.

The back row in the line-out – attack
There are very few attacking opportunities that come a flank forward's way in the course of a line-out other than lending

support, or picking up a stray ball at the end of the line-out. However, a number of line-out variations are used with the flank forward as the leading actor, including shortened line-outs with variations on the throw-in. These include three-men line-outs with the flank at scrum-half. The throw goes over the top to the flank who is supported on the outside by the remaining forwards.

The other variation is the long throw over a shortened line-out to the flank running up from the out-half position. Personally I favour a move often practised by the French at club level, i.e. an ordinary line-out with the exception of the flank who stands beside the out-half. The ball is thrown over the top to the scrum-half who has the support of the flank coming up hard on his outside. From the opposition's point of view this is difficult to cope with – if reasonably executed. The scrum-half is difficult to mark alone, but with the extra man on his outside this can cause all sorts of problems for the defence.

Line-out variations outside the orthodox line-outs depend very much on the thrower's capabilities. The most important thing for him to remember is to throw long rather than short.

Line-out Defence
The line-out has proved to be one of the more unsatisfactory aspects of the modern rugby game. It continues to be a bone of contention with administrations, players and referees. The changes brought about in 1973 by the International Board in a bid to try and rectify a worsening situation appear to have done little for this outstanding problem other than force scrum-halves to pass the ball further than before. It is now slightly more difficult to execute the thousand and one illegalities which exist in almost every line-out and enlarges the gaps which makes defence slightly more hazardous. The main purpose of the change was to try and improve the quality of possession, but this has not been significant.

The rapid advancement of compression has perhaps been

stifled which is just as well, as many of the line-outs on the 1971 Lions tour of New Zealand were near cavalry charges. The application of the methods used in New Zealand have become a little more refined although the basic principles are still implemented. While we were training in Eastbourne prior to our departure to Australia in 1971 we had many discussions on line-out technique. Ray McLoughlin was foremost in these discussions and one of the very first principles adopted to win the line-out was the 'step-across'. It was most important that everyone came across together otherwise it would have been more apparent to referees.

The line-out is a breeding ground for illegalities and here are a few which are used in the name of defence – blocking, jersey pulling, the chain, and generally making a nuisance of yourself. Blocking is the most effective method, done in unison. Sometimes it may be appropriate to use a chain at the back of the line-out, simply linking with the man in front with your arm, thus blocking the spaces. However, it still remains very difficult for the last man in the line-out to block, as there is too much leeway there for his opposite. One can do one of three things, play fair, make a nuisance of yourself or turn laterally across the path of the opposite tail ender when the line-out terminates, thus obstructing his approach to your fly-half.

Basic defence for the scrum-half, out-half and the peel
The last man in the line-out should be given as free a hand as possible. He is however responsible for taking the recipient of the peel ball out of the game before the advantage line is broken. The seventh man in the line-out takes the next man and so on. Sometimes the opposite number moves to No. 8 for the peel ball therefore committing the last man to the jump. Here the seventh man takes the scrum-half break unless of course he has taken a tap from the opposite seventh man.

The fly-half is undoubtedly the most important man to mark off the end of the line-out, so it is important that your own fly-half comes up, rather than hangs back or fades across the pitch. Primarily you are trying to push the fly-half outwards and across and it is therefore important that you do not run directly at him, otherwise you are very susceptible to the side-step. I favour running slightly in front to follow the ball across field and thus keeping very much in the game.

The defensive role of the back row in general terms calls for a very good and clear understanding of each other's roles. It is always made easier from a scrum if the opposition has been given bad ball which limits their options. Back row defence is an important relationship and it is imperative that all eventualities are covered. The back row today tend to hunt together rather than take off in separate directions. It is important, however, that there is depth to their defence, and that one covers the back for possible errors which arise during the course of the game.

Tackling is the main instrument for defence and the first-time tackle is undoubtedly the best. It is important to use both arms and shoulders and lend as much weight as possible to the tackle. The smother tackle is not nearly as effective nor as decisive as felling the man onto the deck.

The Old Enemy, England

GARETH EDWARDS

*Scrum-half, 28, Cardiff and Wales. 40 caps to end 1975
season. Lions 1968–71–74. Played in all Tests 1971–74.*

I have been scoring tries against England since the age of
four. My first memory of rugby was that I *had* to be Wales,
and my younger brother Gethin was left with England. In
Wales the England–Wales rivalry has always been the traditional battle, and even as a child I can remember knowing
when any game between the two countries was going to be
played. There was an electric atmosphere in the valleys.

It is very difficult for outsiders to appreciate the feelings of
the Welsh. If you ask any Welshman which team has to be
overcome during each season it's always England – for a
hundred different reasons. Everyone wants to beat England.
To go to Twickenham and win is great. On the other hand,
Welshmen can't believe they can lose at Cardiff, and when it
happens the nation bleeds. It is not that Welsh people today
feel any inferiority complex (though sometimes we think the
English believe we are still painted up in blue and chucking
spears). It goes back to the past, when the Welsh looked upon
the English as the oppressors and possibly their superiors.
Now that that is all over the only resemblances to those
ancient battles are the annual rugby internationals.

I have heard a thousand explanations why Wales as a
country attaches so much importance to rugby football, but
am still not sure of the true answer. Maybe it gives the people
an identity and is a relief from the hard work.

Because of our social and geographical environment we've
always been a hard-working nation – a nation of steel
workers and coal miners. It's only in recent years that we've

become teachers. People think of Wales as a bleak geo-graphical location, with huge coal tips or steel works, and there is no doubt that in the '20s and '30s life was very hard, and people worked long hours underground. My father went underground when he was fourteen, his father before him when he was 10. They used to go down when it was dark, and it was dark again when they came back up. So when the miners did get the opportunity to go out and see daylight they played games like rugby as a way of unwinding.

I never worked underground, yet I still feel a part of that history without being actually involved. Then there is the language. The great difficulty about the Welsh language is that when translated it loses a lot of impact. The word 'Duw' for instance, directly translated means 'God'. But Duw to a Welshman means a thousandfold 'God, it's hard'.

My parents never taught me my love of rugby. It is some-thing I discovered playing with other children. Older people in the village where I was born, Gwaen-Cae-Gurwen, say that when four or five I played with men of eighteen to twenty. I suspect I was nothing more than a nuisance running in front of them!

A few years later I would play for three or four hours after school, when daylight allowed it, to score a winning try. It didn't matter how long we played for, or whether there were just two of us or four, the winning try always came in the last five minutes, and Wales always won. Somehow or other we always managed to get that result. It speaks a lot for the way we felt, the way we were brought up, and is something you can't really explain unless you are part of that environment. Rugby is the way the Welsh attempt to assert their mas-tery over England. Or at least it has proven so over the years.

We can sing, too, although I'm a nonentity at that. But my father had a lot of ability, like his father and uncles. They were a great singing family and lived in Pencoed, a village about five or six miles from where I was born. Villages in Wales tend to be an identity within themselves. People living only five miles apart are different, even in the way they talk and in their mannerisms.

Although my father has always supported me he was never interested in sport. My grandfather is the only man in my family I can find with any sporting background. He was a rugby player, but better known with his brothers as a musician in the village silver band. I am told he played a solo in front of King George V at the age of twelve. Grandad died in his twenties, leaving my grandmother to bring up three boys – which meant my father never had a chance to follow a singing career. During war service he appeared with stars like Spike Milligan, Harry Secombe and Ken Dodd. I have heard his records, and although they are old and scratched you can tell he had a fine voice.

In Wales the first chance one has of playing representative rugby is at the age of fifteen. District trials are held, but I missed the under-fifteen trial, and so had to wait few a years before I had another chance to represent Wales.

Having missed the earlier opportunity I reverted to soccer, which I had first played when I was twelve, and joined the local team. During that period I was spotted by scouts and was asked to become a professional player with Swansea Town. At the same time, due to the efforts of Bill Samuel, the physical education master at Pontardawe School, I had an opportunity to go to Millfield, the special sports school in Somerset. My parents, being typically Welsh, thought I should pursue my education, and that Millfield, which also had a fine general reputation, was the place for me to go. So off I went. I was a starry-eyed youngster who wanted to be a professional footballer, but I have never regretted attending Millfield. It was there my rugby started again. I joined up with a boy called Vaughan Williams, who was a wonderful schoolboy fly-half. Millfield was a superb team to play in, and had strong fixtures.

Samuel had a tremendous influence on my early sporting career. I could write a book about him and his approach. He was known as a hard man, but he was always admired. At the time I came under him my ambition was to be an athlete and I was training for the long jump and hurdles. Samuel realised the way to get the best out of me was to ridicule and bully me. Automatically I wanted to prove him wrong.

I remember vividly the day at school in 1964 when Wales lost to South Africa 24–3 in Durban. It had been a typical sporting Saturday for me, with an hour's cricket and a lot of running. I was about to join everyone in the changing room when Samuel, who had told me the Durban score, said: 'Edwards, where do you think you're going? You haven't finished yet. I want you to do six 220 yards.' He suggested some ridiculous time, like twenty-four seconds for each. When he took me home that night I was faint and swaying all over the road and cried when I saw my parents. 'He's mad, he's mad,' I said.

Looking back, I realise he was helping by pushing me to the limit. He thought that I had possibly a little more natural ability than the rest. When I used to score sixty- or seventy-yard tries, and returned grinning like a Cheshire cat thinking I was the greatest, he would say: 'No try, you carried the ball in the wrong hand.' This was the way he deflated me in front of my friends, who thought I was the greatest.

He had such a strong influence on me that I remember incidents and conversations as if they were yesterday. For example, we played in Cardiff the morning of the Cardiff–All Blacks in 1963 so we could attend the big match. Although I had set my heart on playing for Wales that ambition seemed a million years away watching such top-class players. During the morning I had scored something like four or five tries, dropped a couple of goals and kicked three penalties. I came off feeling God's gift to the game and all Samuel could say was: 'Do you realise you missed touch twice and gave a hospital pass to your fly-half?' Immediately I was reduced to nothing. He was never satisfied and always setting me new targets.

In the April of 1967, at the age of nineteen, I was selected for Wales against France – only months after leaving school. When I first went out in my red jersey onto the field, I remember bending down and kissing it. Here was something I'd always wanted to achieve. Some players can go through a lifetime and never come near to winning a jersey, and here I was, only nineteen, playing in Paris. Probably because I won my colours so young, I never really appreciated what it meant – not like someone getting his first cap at twenty-nine.

Everybody told me that Colombes Stadium was the worst place on earth to make a debut, yet I was full of confidence and enjoyed every minute. If this was international rugby then I was looking forward to more. Everything happened so quickly that I could not believe it when the final whistle went and Dewi Bebb stuffed the ball up my jersey and said: 'There, keep this as a memento.' France won the game 20–14.

A fortnight later Wales, without a win after three games, were due to play England, who were bidding for the Triple Crown. I was convinced Wales would win. A Welsh commentator who lived nearby asked me to predict the result in a radio interview. Perhaps it was nervousness or an inability to think quickly but I said: 'I tell you something. I think England are going to have a hell of a hiding.' To this day I don't know whether I meant it or it was something I had been brought up to believe every time England played at Cardiff. But England did get a hiding that day – and quite against the odds. It was the time Keith Jarrett scored nineteen points and Wales won 34–21.

The next season the All Blacks came on a medium-length tour. The All Blacks are part of the folklore of Welsh rugby. At school when the weather prevented us playing our master used to read us books about the New Zealanders and told stories of men like Bob Scott, Kel Tremain and Colin Meads. We were given a picture of supermen. Now I found myself playing against them for Wales, and partnering Barry John for the first time in a full game. I felt we could beat them, but in the end we lost – because I think we adopted the wrong tactics.

Near the end of that New Zealand tour I was chosen to captain East Wales against them. The game had to be cancelled because of snow, and was switched to the following Wednesday at Cardiff. That was the early days of Welsh coaching and we had David Hayward helping us. The main team talk took place in a Cardiff pub, the Cockney Pride. Over a bowl of curry we planned how to beat the All Blacks. My idea was that anything that moved had to be tackled, and all loose balls picked up. The boys responded marvellously and we might have won. Whereas New Zealand were a well-coached and organised side we relied on spirit and our fierce will to win. At least we were the only side not to be beaten, as the result was a draw.

My first tour with the Lions was to South Africa in 1968, and it meant that I'd achieved a lifetime within just over a year of leaving school – playing and captaining my country, the Barbarians and now the Lions. It was like entering a new world meeting men like Willie John McBride for the first time, and the captain, Tom Kiernan. These were players I had always looked up to. That taught me a lot, especially how to understand people.

In 1969 Wales won the Triple Crown, which seemed a perfect preparation for our first-ever tour of New Zealand. We thought we were king-pins, but we were in for a rude awakening. The first Test ended in a 19–0 defeat, and was probably the day when, as people say, Barry John and I 'grew up'. We had been billed as 'the best half-back combination in the world', yet we were made to look nonentities. We then lost the second Test 33–12, although I think if it had been played in Cardiff we might have won, which might be difficult to comprehend. That trip made me realise the importance of preparation and team organisation.

Wales achieved the Grand Slam in 1971 on the eve of another Lions tour. That Welsh side had an exceptionally good team and was better prepared than any other because we had been the first to embrace coaching completely. Our preparations had been thorough, which was a distinct advantage over our rivals. We still needed that bit of luck, but if you are good enough you create your own luck. In Murrayfield against Scotland Wales won with the last kick of the match. In the game against Ireland it was desperately hard for the first forty minutes but then we got a break-through and won easily. In the final game we went to France and that, surely, was Wales's finest moment in rugby when we won 9–5.

It was important that year that the Lions started their tour of New Zealand with a winning platform. Whether it was Welsh or Chinese didn't matter. Wales had the nucleus of a winning side which luckily the other nations were prepared to accept and build around. That was the first stepping stone to the success in New Zealand.

Mike Gibson fitted in perfectly with the mainly Welsh back division used by the Lions. But the backs couldn't have functioned properly without the forwards and here Ray McLoughlin sowed the seeds of the destruction of the All Blacks, though his injury cut short his own contribution. Then there were Ian McLauchlan and Sean Lynch who showed determination and grit when they took over the Test prop positions.

John Pullin displayed an attitude which was against his upbringing. He is not an aggressive man, rather placid and typically English, but always stuck to his job as hooker to win the ball. Peter Dixon was another Englishman who impressed me tremendously. McBride took over the forward leadership when McLoughlin departed and was the man who kept the pack together. McBride proved to certain Press critics that he was not over the hill.

As a Welsh Lion to have played in a team which beat New Zealand in a Test series for the first time this century, it gave me tremendous pleasure, especially after the disappointment in 1969. Then Barry John and myself were described as being a waste of time. 'How dare they send these babies to play against the might of New Zealand?' it was said. One New Zealand critic wrote of me: 'Not a bad player, but he believes too much in his own write-ups.' I won't say we stuffed the words down the critics' mouths, but at least Barry and myself proved we had some ability and this gave us a lot of pleasure.

I tend to play most of my rugby in fear – not fear of injury but fear over whether the opposition performs better than us. Playing and winning well gave me tremendous satisfaction. When appearing before big international crowds, especially at Cardiff Arms Park, I want them to remember what they are seeing, and remember it as one of their own great experiences.

An outstanding example of this came in 1973, when the Barbarians took on the All Blacks at Cardiff Arms Park. It was obviously going to be a showdown. The Barbarians side included most of the members of the victorious 1971 Lions team who had been hero-worshipped all through the four home countries. The New Zealanders had come for their revenge: they had been successful against the home countries and had now reached the end of a long tour.

It was a beautiful day. The crowd were in an exceptional mood, as if they sensed something was going to happen. The first two minutes quickly vanished and my mouth was dry with the nervousness which overcomes everyone in such circumstances. I was forced to challenge Bryan Williams, who received a pass from Ian Kirkpatrick following a blind side break. Williams hooked the ball down towards our posts and I thought: 'What did he want to do that for?' I was already feeling the pace and had to force my legs to run backwards to cover when I saw Phil Bennett scampering back towards our posts, being chased by three All Blacks.

I thought he was bound to kick the ball for touch, but for no apparent reason he sidestepped back inside, beating all three men. On the film you see me covering back, as Phil is coming forward infield towards the south stand. By then I was somewhere between the 25 and the half way line. Surprised that he hadn't kicked, I didn't really know what to do. On film movements appear to be fast but during the game they are slower, unfolding in front of you. Phil passed the ball to J. P. R. Williams, who rode a tackle before passing to John Pullin. As Pullin is unaccustomed to such a situation, everyone expected him to kick to touch and kill the ball there and then. Instead he passed on to John Dawes, who ran past me as I was going in the other direction. Everything was now happening behind me.

As I turned round to attempt to join the move my legs felt like lead. I was breathing hard and my mouth was dry. All I wanted somebody to do was put the ball to touch so the game could settle down. I was frightened we would do something daft early in the game. I saw Dawes sidestep two men and break infield passing to Tommy David. I still could not understand what was going on fifteen yards ahead, but then I thought something could happen and decided to chase. The crowd were beginning to sense something momentous was about to take place. They had been lifted by Phil Bennett not having killed the ball, by his failure to conform.

Four Barbarians had handled the ball within our 25. So everything everybody had hoped for had already begun to happen within two minutes of the kick-off. Tommy David now brought off a superb one-handed pass to Derek Quinnell, who somehow managed to take the ball below his knees. I only remained with the play because it is the scrum-half's job to be up for any breakdown. I was frightened what would happen if the ball went loose and I was not there to pick it up. It's funny looking back on it that I was there running in support mainly because I didn't want to make a fool of myself. Most of what happened in the closing stages of that try are a blur. I remember Quinnell being tackled and just throwing the ball to his left. I managed to take it and had the sensation I was running faster than ever before in my life. Although I was oblivious to the crowd I could hear the background murmur. There were still thirty yards to go to the line, but as I went past the first defender I knew nobody was going to catch me. It didn't matter if I had to run to Newport, I was not going to be caught. I just had to score. When I finally slammed the ball down it was a tremendous feeling.

186

Soccer players turn to the crowd and salute after scoring but I feel embarrassed by this sort of display and have no desire to run round the field saying: 'I'm the greatest'. Some of the team – I remember Fergus Slattery, Mike Gibson, Gerald Davies and David Duckham in particular – came up and congratulated me, but I was only the final figure in a movement that will be regarded as having led to one of rugby's immortal tries.

Afterwards I had difficulty believing it had really happened and wondered 'are we all going to wake up?' It was the finest game in which I have ever played. I would rate the third Test in New Zealand in 1971 and the third Test in South Africa in 1974 as more important, but for excitement the Barbarians game at Cardiff excelled. I also admired the way the New Zealanders came back. At one stage we were seventeen points up. By then you might have thought the All Blacks would have given up, yet at one stage I thought they might even win.

Before the 1974 Lions tour I had been around long enough to be written off. There were young scrum-halves coming up in Wales and some people didn't think I was good enough even to play for Cardiff. Although I had enjoyed all the victories rugby has to offer, I was still motivated. I had to prove to people who said I was not good enough. Perhaps I had the voice of Bill Samuel at the back of my mind.

The control shown by those 1974 forwards was unbelievable. In New Zealand the Lions pack achieved a compromise, pinched possibly thirty to forty per cent of the ball, and won with the help of some exceptional backs. In South Africa the forwards were so superior they dominated the scene. The strength and determination was such that whenever we held the ball in the scrum the opposition was unable to function. I would say: 'Right boys, keep it going, superb, put it a bit right, left a bit, put it here,' and their control was so perfect that I could look round, judge the South African defensive placings, and then take the ball out at will.

I was very wary when we approached the first Test in Cape Town because I remembered a similar match in Pretoria six years earlier when I thought the Lions could not lose. Then we had won seven games on the trot, having faced most of the men who were in the Springbok Test side. Yet still we lost 25–20. That might not sound too poor a performance, but anyone who was present knows we were badly blasted. I realised in 1974 that these Lions were a better team, but I was afraid that South Africa would produce something akin to that day in Pretoria. What I didn't foresee was that the Springboks had lost confidence. On one occasion Ian McCallum tried to kick a penalty from seventy yards out in the mud; it was not even a good kick.

In the first half of that first Test the Lions were playing against a strong wind, but the Springboks never looked like getting a try – although they led with a dropped goal. We looked far more dangerous and this was encouraging because in the second half the elements were in our favour and a good kick could gain sixty yards. By the second half the Lions pack was completely dominant. It was bliss playing behind them. The Springbok pack was going back all the time.

The second Test was played at Pretoria and this is where I thought the Springboks would put their backs to the wall and die rather than be taken prisoners. It didn't happen like that, maybe because there had been so many changes in their team, and the Lions were much better prepared. South Africa also missed their early penalty goals while we scored with our first chance. After we had scored again I knew it was virtually over. The second half was a formality and the myth of South Africa's invincibility at Pretoria was broken.

They then had to win the third Test to save the series, and certainly played better than in the previous two. Yet they missed their early chances. You cannot let opportunities slip in Test matches. I was slightly injured and did not play well but had to survive the match. If I went off Tony Neary would have had to take my place because the other scrum-half, John Moloney, was injured. It was a hard first half but the turning point was when Gordon Brown scored from a line-out just before the interval. This completely demoralised the Springboks. Later Andy Irvine kicked a penalty goal from the half way line and there was nothing could stop us winning the series.

After the match I felt very much as I did following the fourth Test in New Zealand. It was an anti-climax. The pressure had been so great before the match, but when it was all over it seemed disappointing. It was satisfying to think we had made Willie John and Syd Millar happy, because they had given so much. It was also nice to think about my wife, Maureen, and my son who in the years to come would say: 'My dad went to South Africa in 1974'. We had achieved something, and there were so many people at home who'd be proud of us.

The Scrum-Half

GARETH EDWARDS

Any scrum-half needs to be able to kick with both feet, employ a variety of passes, and be strong enough to take a lot of buffeting from forwards and break a tackle near the scrum. When I was a schoolboy I would practise the basic skills for hours. My physical education master would roll the ball to my left and right and tell me to kick or pass in one movement. Then he would have players jumping at me so that I worked under pressure. This is essential, because the scrum-half is seldom free of attention from the opposition.

Nowadays I do not have the same time to train, except on tour, but it is important to maintain one's skills. I always practise ten minutes before or after a club training session. It helps to be gymnastically minded. Fortunately I have always been enthusiastic about gymnastics and it has helped me have a body-awareness in mid-air. As a scrum-half you end up in all sorts of positions, but the key is to get the ball away safely. Often when the ball comes out of a line-out an opponent comes through and you have to ride the tackle just as you are stretched to pass. Strength is thus a major asset, and I am grateful that I did weight-training between the ages of fourteen and seventeen. You need to be strong to recover quickly after being hit, or from being held when attempting to pass or kick.

QUALITY POSSESSION

I have had many arguments with leading coaches on the question of what constitutes quality scrum possession. Ray Williams, the Welsh coaching organiser, argues that the best possession from the scrum comes when the ball emerges between the prop and flanker on the near side of the put-in because it is quick. This sounds ideal, but in practice doesn't work because the scrum-half is under constant pressure from his opposite number – that is, unless it's perfectly channelled. You have to be in your stride almost immediately after putting the ball in, and that is difficult.

I prefer a slow heel, even if many coaches say this defeats the object in view. On the 1974 Lions' tour a lock would stop the ball and move it across the scrum to the No. 8, who then placed it on his right – the far side of the scrum from where the ball was put in. In those circumstances no scrum-half worth his salt should be caught: he receives controlled ball and is unlikely to put his fly-half under pressure. Of course, a scrum-half has to be equipped to deal with a ball which just shoots out.

TACTICAL APPRECIATION

Knowing when to pass, kick or break comes with experience. A young player tends to do any one of these things at the wrong times and often in the wrong order. It is a matter of understanding the conditions of the match at any particular moment. Bill Samuel used to say: 'You don't break at 3.30 p.m. and kick to touch at 3.45 p.m. It depends on the situation.'

I found my first season in senior rugby the best because no one knew my capabilities and I was often able to catch them unaware. The next season the opposition knew more about me and were able to exert more pressure. I still often try to lull the opposition into believing I can't do certain things. I play the game by the way I feel rather than by the text book. Often I have been in situations when I have been convinced I have made the right decision, but afterwards good critics in the stand say I should have done something else.

A player sees the game in a different way from someone in the stand. Opponents also see the game differently. After a

Cardiff–Llanelli club game, Llanelli's Lions flanker Tom David said: 'Oh, I hammered you. You never came near me once.' He was right – but it was because I knew it would have been suicide. Tom stood off the scrum every time, so I kicked between him and the wing, or between him and the scrum, and gained thirty to fifty yards at a time. That's game appreciation – realising that to run would be suicidal and finding another method of attack.

My advice is never go looking for a break. Wait for it, even if you have to wait until another game. The moment you start looking will be the time you get caught. Even here, though, one cannot make strict rules. During the 1971 tour of New Zealand I discarded this advice against Otago and made a break, which led to a try by John Dawes. Although I hate thinking what to do in a match I felt against Otago something had to be done to end the deadlock. That is why I forced a break and fortunately it succeeded.

THE FLY-HALF

It is important to know your partner. Barry John liked to stand still and take the ball deep, rather than run on to a pass. Phil Bennett stands deep but takes the ball in front, going flat out. Mike Gibson is similar to John as he likes to get the ball first and then think out the move. You would call both John and Gibson instinctive players. Yet everything depends on the type of ball received by the scrum-half because this determines what chance the fly-half has of launching a successful attack.

I have often been asked how I developed the spin pass. When I first played for Wales at the age of nineteen my passing was frequently criticised and I realised I would have to improve to survive as an international. No doubt I was influenced by the passing of Ken Catchpole of Australia and Chris Laidlaw of New Zealand. I watched Laidlaw a lot and decided to persevere with the spin pass. Although slower it is more accurate.

Quality possession

8. *From a line-out:* the Lions' forwards in New Zealand protect Gareth Edwards from the All Blacks' pack and he is able to send out a boom pass to Barry John

9. *From the set scrum:* perfect ball has been delivered from the pack and again Gareth Edwards has all the time he needs to prepare an attack, unmolested by the Springbok opposition. This photograph was taken during the fourth Test and behind Gareth Edwards can be seen Max Baise, the controversial referee

Defence and attack

10. Mervyn Davies illustrates a perfect smother tackle as he gets a hand on the ball carried by All Black, Ian Kirkpatrick. Behind Davies is Peter Dixon, up in support, while Sid Going (right) looks on

11. Line-outs frequently become mauls and allow the opportunity for setting up an attack. Here, in the third Test against South Africa, Gordon Brown is in possession. Support is given by Bobby Windsor (left), Roger Uttley (right) and McBride, who is directly behind Brown

It was a help when I was selected to go to South Africa with the Lions in 1968. During the three months out there in superb conditions I had plenty of time to practise. A spin pass is pretty straightforward, like a one-handed pass. One hand is taken sharply across the ball, causing it to spin, and the other is used as a guide. It's very simple even if it sounds complicated. I sometimes use the reverse pass in certain situations and it can be effective, but it has a large element of risk.

POSITIONING

Balance, and knowing where the fly-half is standing, is the key to positioning. Basically you want to pass with the least amount of body movement, like hitting a golf ball. If I am facing the wrong way to my fly-half I am forced to make two movements, and this wastes time. From a line-out the positioning is automatically different, because the fly-half has to stand ten yards back. Personally this law helps me, because I find it easier to pass from a line-out than from a scrum. From a scrum the ball is on the ground and I usually use the dive pass. You need to be on your feet to throw a spin pass. From a scrum you are usually under more pressure and the diving action puts more distance between the opposition and the ball.

BACK ROW SUPPORT

The New Zealanders have always been masters of this type of support. We all know that the shortest distance between two points is a straight line, and that is how Syd Going attempts to break the gain line. Once over and tackled he just flicks the ball over his head, under his legs or to his side. He has been backed up by such fine back row forwards as Kel Tremain, Brian Lochore, Ian Kirkpatrick or Waka Nathan, and he knows one of these will be there to pick up the ball.

I was also taught at an early age that fly-halves must be

nursed. Fly-half protection is also important for the rest of the back division, because bad ball from a scrum-half becomes even worse when pushed along the line. If the fly-half is knocked about or under pressure then the efficiency of the team soon breaks down. Again it is a matter of match appreciation, learning when to kick rather than shovel out rubbishy ball. In most of the games Phil Bennett and I played for Wales in 1974 we were under pressure, and often in desperation I had to give out poor ball and hope that his ability would save the situation.

The forward I love having on my side is Dai Morris. We used to have a great laugh when Wales introduced proper coaching, with complicated rules about where everyone should go after a scrum break. Dai's words to me were: 'You run and I'll be with you.' Hence his nickname 'The Shadow' – it didn't matter where I went, Dai would be with me. This support is what every scrum-half looks for. On many occasions you act instinctively – you might see a break and have no time to tell anyone. You look an idiot if tackled after twenty yards without support, but the same burst becomes a tremendous movement if the ball can be flicked to a flank forward.

DEFENCE FROM SET-SCRUM, RUCK AND MAUL

Now that the laws say both scrum-halves must stand on the same side as the ball is put in, I tend to follow the ball around initially, trying to harrass my opposite number. If I find the ball is being well controlled by the opposition I quickly retreat and go back to cover behind our back line or on the blind side, depending on which way the opposition is about to move. But if the opposing team's possession is poor then I try to force the other scrum-half into making a mistake. From a maul or a ruck the scrum-half takes a position on the blind side with the last forward up policing the open side to cut off any attack.

ATTACK FROM RUCK OR MAUL

It is difficult to attack effectively from a static-maul position because it is like a set-scrum, with a similar defence pattern. It is important to work for a situation where the defence are going backwards and the opposing flank forwards are forced to tie themselves into the scrum. This is called the 'dynamic ruck-maul', and is an ideal attacking platform. Then you have the element of surprise which is needed in rugby. When the opposition forwards are trying desperately to hold the fort the attacking scrum-half normally finds himself in the situation which demands that he runs. From a static maul-ruck you either kick or pass to the fly-half, leaving him to decide on the next move. Alternatively, your forwards can break, starting a new maul-ruck to create better ball.

Passing bad ball from a maul or ruck can be very danger-ous for the fly-half, because he is in danger of being badly hurt by a flanker travelling at speed. It is better for the scrum-half to take the knocks himself, because they are un-likely to be so severe. Scrum-halves also become more hardened because of all the work needed around the scrum. It is partly tradition, but there's a lot of sense in it as well.

I would like to end by explaining why nine- or ten-man rugby has become so common in major games. When a game is important mistakes must be eliminated, but errors are always likely when spinning the ball about among the backs. With efficient half-backs ground can be made to help gain an attacking position near the opposition line. There is a ten-dency to believe that the 1971 Lions always played fifteen-man rugby, but this only happened when we were allowed to do so. Often the 1971 team played in the ten- or nine-man style. If you are against a side which is determined to break down your three-quarter play, and to prey off your mistakes, it is suicidal to throw the ball around just to please the crowds and satisfy your critics.

It is true that the 1971 Lions were better equipped than

the 1974 team when the situation arose, but it was also
determined by the opposition. The New Zealanders at least
often tried to run the ball themselves, while in 1974 the
South Africans were only concerned with smashing down
movements. The only way to counteract this was to put the
ball behind them.

Pressure Produces Players

MIKE GIBSON

Centre, fly-half, 31, North of Ireland and Ireland, 51 caps to end 1975 season. Lions 1966–68–71–74.
Played in four Tests 1971–74.

Sport has always been a major passion in my life, and during my early days this interest was expressed through soccer. This was quite natural, as relations had played the game at the highest level and my parents travelled each Saturday to watch an Irish League match. In short I could scarcely avoid sport: it dominated our household. At preparatory school I was introduced to organised soccer for the first time and for a couple of years all my energies were applied to soccer. Work was a distraction – although I should add that the priorities were observed after the initial attraction! I wanted to be involved in all sports. At soccer inside forward was the ideal position because it demanded attack and defence and at cricket I was an opening batsman and wicket keeper, always hoping I could remain on the field of play throughout the match. I suppose this desire for activity has created in me a serious approach to all sport and an attitude of never being satisfied with inferior standards.

My prep. school rugby career started at scrum-half. A partnership with my elder brother, Peter, ended when he advanced to Campbell College, and, eager to equal him, I moved to fly-half for the Cabin Hill 1st XV.

Eventually I went on to Campbell College, a school with a long tradition in rugby, but I never abandoned my interest in soccer. Even to this day if there is an opportunity to play soccer – which often arises on Lions tours, particularly with people like Barry John around – I am glad of the chance to return, if briefly, to my first love.

My main interest in the Saturday sports results has always been the soccer results, particularly the fortunes of Newcastle United. I have followed them since I was nine, enjoyed their successes in the '50s and suffered with them through the '60s. At the age of thirteen I had ambitions to play soccer professionally, but in fact I have had so much enjoyment out of rugby that I never really gave serious consideration to deciding between the two games. Soccer has enormous attractions, but I am very satisfied with rugby. I enjoy participation in all sports ranging from athletics to tennis, with golf my principal activity when I am away from a rugby field. I have a single figure handicap, with the ambition of reducing it once my rugby-playing days are at an end. Thank goodness my wife enjoys sport too!

I have been fortunate enough to play international rugby both as fly-half and centre. The former position is more demanding, as it is pivotal to the rest of the game, but each position gives equal pleasure. At fly-half there is the involvement, attracting attention from both the opposite fly-half and back row, and in the centre there is the freedom to express oneself. If anyone had a licence to run it must be in midfield, and I have enjoyed myself immensely at all levels when playing at centre – especially with a fly-half who sets up the moves. In the centre you have the thrill of supporting a move and being able to stay close to the ball.

Before I embark on the techniques for backplay I want to stress the importance of the forwards. Having played behind beaten packs I have been able to appreciate any possession received, realising the need to put it to the right use. As Lions' backs, we had to struggle in New Zealand in 1966, and enjoyed but occasional success in South Africa in 1968. With the advent of coaching in the '70s we started to get better ball, and this transformed the possibilities of our back play.

Throughout the home countries, possession has now emerged as the be-all and end-all. In acknowledging this aim coaches have concentrated on the techniques of doing the simple things well. Those very principles apply throughout the game – to backs as well as forwards.

Just as coaching and organisation have improved the playing side of the game, the legislators have done their share by compelling defences to lie back ten yards, so giving the backs, in theory, more time to attempt moves and to make the game more attractive to both players and spectators. Yet I believe this is a double-edged weapon. Although it might allow players greater freedom it removes the intense pressure, and so allows them to get away with a lower standard of skill. Certainly pressure exposes a player, and shows whether he has the right to be an international or is an imposter. That is why I stress the importance of practising under pressure situations.

The Three-quarter's Skills

MIKE GIBSON

The most vital consideration in rugby – winning possession –
has been covered by other contributors. For backs the prime
consideration is to make the best use of the ball provided.
All their training, both physical and mental, must go towards producing the correct answer to the given situation.
And practice is the constant theme which should run through
any discussion of the various options.

It sometimes seems that the greater freedom given to
three-quarters by the changes in the laws has been used to
develop the art of kicking. Here practice enables a player to
develop a sound technique to improve the judgment of when
to use a particular kick and to attain accuracy. Practice also
breeds confidence.

Kicking skills are similar to certain skills in golf. As with a
golf stroke, so the kicker must be well balanced, must keep
his eye on the ball before impact, must follow through and
must realise that the crowd will let him know the result of
his kick; there will then be no need for him to follow the
flight of a ball prematurely.

Practice also helps a player to be able to kick with either
foot. This is a point of massive importance, as to be restricted
to one side greatly limits a player's options. There have been
instances of great players who were thus restricted but a
study of them would probably reveal they had other com-
pensating factors, such as speed or footwork, so that they
could manoeuvre into a position where they could use their
favoured foot.

ATTACKING KICKS

First, there is the high kick to the post. There are two methods of making this kick. There is a screw kick, when a ball is angled slightly in the hands, and is then dropped across the instep with the player leaning back slightly to allow speedy elevation. This type of kick is not affected very much by the wind, and thus its flight is reasonably predictable. It also has the merit of causing the ball to accelerate in its later stages: the ball can spiral slightly, like a shell fired from a gun which tails off at the end of its flight, and this can cause difficulty to the full-back or to the player placed underneath.

The second method is to strike the ball in the middle with the seam facing the point of target, or even with the ball turned sideways, and the foot striking straight through. This causes the ball to waver and drift in its flight, again creating difficulties for defenders. This sort of kick can be used by a three-quarter outside his own 25 as a type of Garryowen. If the ball was held in the cross position it would tend to back-spin in the air and drift for longer than the screw kick, so giving the attacking players more time to chase. This kick is made with a slightly restricted follow-through, so that there is little break in the stride pattern of the kicker.

The second type of attacking kick is that placed behind an opposing wing. The high kick can be used with similar principles to those of the high kick to the posts, or the flighted kick can be performed in two ways. First there is the screw kick, with the ball angled across the instep to the ground and struck hard. This produces a deceptive flight which tends to cheat the elements and causes difficulty to the defending wing when he tries to estimate its speed. This type of kick will tend to skid on impact with the ground.

The other flighted kick I would advocate is with no screw applied, the ball being struck down the middle line with a long follow-through. The result is a wavering flight, with the ball spinning end over end, and on striking the ground it runs forward in an unpredictable way, thereby improving the chances of confusing the defence.

Another kick open to three-quarters is the short attacking type. This can again be done in two ways. The first is a grubber kick, with the ball being dropped on to the foot. It is struck with the toe pointed almost straight to the ground so that the ball bounces forward, with the possibility of sitting up for an attacker to gather in his stride. However, I do not favour this kick as it requires almost a big enough gap in the opposition's defence to allow a player to run through. The unpredictable bounce can also fool the attacker.

I prefer the chip kick, gently stroking the ball over the heads of advancing defenders and into an open space. Naturally there is the risk of this kick being charged down, but with practice this risk is reduced enormously. Also the chip, when well done, will produce more opportunities for an attacking player to gather the ball out of the air without any noticeable slackening of speed. The kick is done with the foot turned upwards slightly and with little follow-through. It is a gentle but firm tap of the ball.

There are other types of attacking kick, namely the one into the box and the cross kick, but the principles detailed above apply to both these options. Do remember, though, that with any kick it is the actual *kick* that has priority. Many players run too fast and are unbalanced when attempting these rather difficult kicks.

DEFENCE KICKS

The general principles here are quite straightforward. The first essential is to find touch and not to be too ambitious. No team-mate appreciates an attempt at a forty-five-yard touch kick which fails and puts the team under pressure. It is better to lower your sights and guarantee that the object is achieved. Once that principle is firmly in your mind then set about discovering the distance you are capable of kicking. Leading players tend to make full use of each defensive kick and not to waste thirty yards with the ball flying over the crowd.

HANDLING

By tradition this is the real purpose and distinguishing feature of the game. Again it is important to practise so that skills become second nature, and the mind does not have to worry about dropping passes. Just as a professional golfer has to concentrate on something simple, like his grip, the rugby player must not allow his mind to be detracted from the first requirement of catching the ball. When this is achieved then the mind is free to decide what best to do.

Catching is the starting point, and when this skill has been developed the ball becomes an extension of your arms. Practising in groups, one can concentrate on sharpness, slip-catching or throwing difficult passes. The more the ball is used, the better the player is likely to be as he develops confidence. Correct alignment and positional play are vital in any movement, and frequently poor anticipation can cause good handling to come to nothing. Practice and discipline are the essential qualities here. Remember, it is better to err on the side of being too far behind the ball carrier. You are of no value in front of him.

Once you have mastered the ability to catch the ball the next step is to pass the ball on. Here it is the end result which is important and not strictly the method used.

The first method of passing is the traditional pass, with the weight of one's body swung away from the intended recipient. This involves putting the weight on to the foot furthest from the catcher and consequently the body will turn naturally, presenting the hip to a prospective tackler. The hands swing across the line of the extended hip, and a follow-through is necessary to guide the ball to the target. There are many merits in this type of passing. First, it compels concentration. Second, it has the effect of straightening the attacking line. Third, it is the natural precursor to a dummy. Fourth, the defender has to pay attention to the attacker, which prevents him being in a position to cover.

The second method is the wrist pass, which involves a short, sharp flick movement to transfer the ball to the target as quickly as possible. The natural merits of this type of pass are the speed at which it can be given and the opportunities it creates for support. The defects are reasonably obvious. There is a greater risk of fault, it requires more concentration, and it depends on the giver of the pass having first received the ball in a correct position.

An essential aspect of passing, obviously, is that the ball must be put in front of the receiver. Once that is done everything becomes possible in attack. It is a wonderful sight in rugby when the ball is spun along the three-quarter line and each pass beats closing tacklers.

Rugby would be an improved spectacle if the game comprised uninterrupted quality with points being earned by greater ability. Regrettably, defects play a substantial role. The blemishes may be of a cerebral nature involving lack of appreciation and vision but frequently they are simple faults that could be corrected by practice. Luckily I had the benefit of excellent coaching at the formative stage of my rugby career, but too often players of talent are permitted to acquire and develop faults. These faults are common to the game regardless of the level, be it coarse rugby or international rugby.

For example, study any fly-half. Note his positional play, remembering his role as the initiator of almost all the movements. If his team is under pressure you will frequently see him moving behind the set-piece instead of holding his correct position. This is simply self-protection. The fly-half may gain comfort by directing the play but such positioning reduces the possibilities open to his side. Once he adopts such a position he is compelled to run across the field and the rest of the backs have no option but to follow.

Another defect concerns his state of mind. A fly-half can become so self-important that he considers he must do something as an individual with each ball he receives. He then neglects his role as a link and so neglects his side. To succeed at the highest level the fly-half also requires absolute concentration. Once his mind wanders or he becomes determined to achieve individual supremacy over a wing-forward or his opposite number, his appreciation of any situation wanes, and he becomes less alert to new possibilities.

The faults of a fly-half are easy to see and often have a greater effect than errors made by his fellow backs, but the principles involved when discussing a fly-half's defects apply equally to the backs as a whole. Watch a centre in action. Often he feels he *must* make a break, and even makes it *before* the ball arrives. This is stupid play; it is better to go through an entire match without a clean break than to waste possession with a futile attempt to force a break. Proper centre play involves rapid appreciation of the options on receipt of the ball, but too often a centre will expose his mental limitations by simply stampeding at the opposition, allegedly setting up a 'risk situation'. This method can sometimes work, but recently it has become the standard play of the centre who is heavy – both physically and mentally! With that style it means the centre can retain his place in a side *ad nauseam*, as nothing drastic can happen provided he holds on to the ball having set up the risk. The finger of blame can often be pointed at the coach, with his overwhelming desire to cross the gain line at the earliest possible opportunity. Also a centre must resist the temptation to measure his contribution to a match by adding up the number of occasions on which he had the better of his opposite number. To become involved in a duel within a match results in wasted possession, with a centre running across the field in an attempt to create a break and tucking the ball under one arm, so advertising his intention of making an individual sortie.

A centre should master the simple arts of rugby and recognise his role as a supporter of movement. He should be willing, in other words, to do more running in support than in possession. Compare rugby with the world of commerce. No business could provide a better return for investment than rugby. The rewards are the product of the effort.

It's Frightening Watching Myself on Television

J. P. R. WILLIAMS

Full-back, 26, London Welsh and Wales. 32 caps to end of
1975 season. Lions 1971–74. Played in all Tests.

As a youngster I was encouraged to be an attacking full-back, which meant that the 'no kicking outside the defensive 25' laws introduced in 1968–69 played into my lap. I first really understood the advantages of attacking from the rear during my year at school at Millfield, in Somerset, where it was school policy. We also played in a lot of seven-a-side competitions, and this improved my running with the ball. From school I played for my home town club, Bridgend, who have always put the emphasis on attacking rugby. I played with them in the Floodlit Alliance, where only tries counted, so it was essential for everyone to join in attacks.

I always had a good eye for a ball, and this plus a little skill helped me win the Wimbledon junior tennis title in 1966. I have often wondered what I might have achieved if I had followed a tennis career to the full. After leaving Millfield and going to medical school in London, however, I had to choose between tennis or rugby. Tennis is a full-time sport now, but by choosing rugby I still had enough 'spare time' to study and qualify.

Yet my tennis background has been a tremendous influence on my rugby career. Playing tennis taught me to watch the ball all the time, which is important when opposing forwards are bearing down on you and you have to take a high kick. The important skill is to shut the oncoming players out of your mind and concentrate on the ball in the air. When you start thinking about being hit it's time to pack it in.

Rugby has been part of my life since the age of five, when I first played for Laleston Primary School as a wing. This was my position until the age of eleven, when I joined Bridgend Grammar School and switched to full-back. From then on I scaled the ladder in the same way as many Welsh internationals, by playing for the Welsh schools national under-15 team and Welsh secondary schools team. I had already played for Bridgend by the time I was eighteen and joined St Mary's Hospital, London.

In 1968 I was chosen to tour Argentina with Wales, and this was to have a major influence on my career as I met John Dawes, who persuaded me to play for London Welsh. At the time the club concentrated a hundred per cent on attack, and it was a wonderful experience playing with so many talented attacking players. The forwards were not very big, which meant we were always struggling for possession, but what we did get was exploited to the full. Everyone in the side attained an amazing level of fitness, and whatever was lacking in size was more than made up for in energy and skill.

I have always enjoyed the physical aspect of the game. At school I was tiny, smaller even than Phil Bennett with whom I appeared in the Welsh under-15 team. I think this taught me courage, as I was often forced to face opponents who were much bigger. The big match temperament I learnt from my days in top-class tennis when I was on my own in front of large crowds. I sometimes get quite frightened when I watch myself on television, but on the field at the time I do what I consider correct. My philosophy has always been that the harder you play and go into tackle, the less chance you have of being injured. I have always loved rugby, but consider it is essential always to play to win. After all, it is a competitive game and there has to be a winner. So why be a loser? This has been the big change in attitude to Lions rugby – the will to win, which has been somewhat lacking in past sides.

Comparing the tours to New Zealand and South Africa is impossible, as the opposition and climatic conditions were so vastly different. However, things were made easier for the

Stars in New Zealand

2. David Duckham, the fair-headed English wing, excited New Zealand crowds with his pace and his ability to elude tackles. Here he takes on Bruce Hunter during the third Test, with All Blacks' centre, Howard Joseph, also hot in pursuit

3. Gerald Davies was another who tormented New Zealand by his ability to change direction at top speed. He is seen here scoring one of the four tries against Hawkes Bay, leaving two rivals on the deck

. . . and in South Africa

14. J. P. R. Williams symbolised the new breed of Lions: courageous, fearless and a supreme competitor. He is making a break during the closing moments of the fourth Test

15. One of the most exciting young Lions during the tour was Scottish full-back Andy Irvine, seen here on his way to scoring a try against Natal

16. Finally, Mike Gibson in full flight. He has now played on four Lions tours and is rated by good judges to be the best all-round back in the world since the war

three-quarters in South Africa as we won much more of the ball. In New Zealand the Lions had only about forty per cent possession in the Tests, whereas it was probably nearer sixty per cent in South Africa. This meant that the 1971 team had to rely more on their backs to make the best use of limited possession. Consequently they often produced brilliant attacking rugby, and scored some of the best tries in which it has been my privilege to be involved. Teams naturally play to their strength, and I would say the Lions' strength in New Zealand was mainly among the backs while in South Africa it was in the forwards. Yet it would be wrong to under-estimate the 1974 back line, which played an important part in a Test team producing ten tries in four games – five in the second Test.

Controversial incidents are as much a part of the life of a top-class rugby player as any other sportsman, and I have had a fair number of them. The most distressing concerned Tommy Bedford, Oxford Blue, Natal and ex-Springbok captain, when the 1974 Lions were playing Natal a week after winning the Test series in Port Elizabeth. The Lions felt proud of their achievement – justifiably, I think. However, the South African newspapers were full of how Natal were going to beat us, and why Tommy Bedford should be captain of the Springboks, so much so that by the time we got to Durban we were fed up with the sound of Natal, and Tommy Bedford.

Although Phil Bennett put the Lions ahead after a couple of minutes with a penalty goal it was a hard game, due to Natal's tremendous tackling and stamina. Mid-way through the second half there was a kick into our 25. I slightly fumbled the ball, though keeping it behind me, and finally I was knocked into touch by Tommy Bedford and my Lions colleague Mervyn Davies. When falling I was kicked in the back of my head. This made me furious and I must admit I lost my temper. I lashed out two or three times at Bedford on the ground, and he lay there as if unconscious. The incident took place close to spectators, and I thought the whole crowd was going to attack me. Phil Bennett was on the spot and was convinced that Bedford hadn't been knocked out. Certainly he was on his feet a couple of minutes later and running about as if nothing had happened. After the tour finished I worked a few months in Durban, and for a long time it seemed the whole of Natal hated me, as Bedford is their rugby idol.

Another incident on the South African tour was in the fourth Test when the Springboks put up a high kick for their forwards. I managed to jump and take the ball, but was immediately dumped on the floor. Someone then gave me an almighty kick at the back of my head. This started some trouble among the packs, and later I learned that it was 'Moaner' Van Heerden who was the culprit. He and I had been having a mini-feud throughout the series, and this was his idea of getting his own back – by kicking me when I was on the ground. At least the Lions won a penalty from it all, which relieved a tight defensive situation.

The Lions tour of New Zealand in 1971 also brings memories of bruising incidents. The vital third Test at Wellington was only five minutes old when a high kick was put up to Barry John, with the whole All Black pack descending. I could see what would happen if he took the ball, so as I am two and a half stone heavier I came forward and took over. As I caught the ball and turned my back I felt a simultaneous thud in both buttocks, where two of the New Zealand forwards had come in with their knees. It was four days before I could sit down again. But Barry John could well have been off the field for good if he had taken that ball; as it was he went on to score ten points and win the all-important match for us.

The fourth Test included an enjoyable incident from my point of view. Jass Muller, a member of the All Black front row, fairly unpopular for his dubious tactics, came round the front of a line-out with the ball and charged towards me. It was a case of a 14 st. full-back challenging a $17\frac{1}{2}$ st. prop forward in a bid to stop a try. I managed to time a shoulder-barge just right, so that he bounced off me on to his back into touch. I can still remember the look on his face as he hit the deck with a great exhalation of breath. Colin Meads, who was captaining New Zealand, told me that evening that Muller had said on his way to the ensuing line-out, 'Dirty player, that Williams.' Coming from Muller it was quite an amusing comment . . . a sort of pot calling the kettle All Black.

Back Line Attacks

J. P. R. WILLIAMS

Even though I am an attacking full-back (and was criticised earlier on in my career for being too adventurous) I believe that the full-back's first job is to be the last line of defence. The basics of full-back play, fielding high kicks, clearing to touch and tackling, still apply as much as they ever did. However, the full-back's game no longer stops there. He is ideally placed to join in an attack, because he is positioned behind the three-quarters and can therefore enter the line at much greater pace than either of the centres. And there is nobody automatically marking him.

I normally enter the line between the outside centre and the wing. This, if performed properly, leaves me and my wing against the opposing wing. If he comes in to tackle me, I pass to my wing to put him away on the overlap. If the opposing wing stays and shadows his opposite number then I go on my own and either score a try myself, pass inside to the back row, or if tackled create a ruck or maul situation for second phase possession. For the full-back to participate in this sort of move it is vital that the blind side wing comes across the field behind the three-quarter line to act as substitute full-back. This obviously caters for any handling mistakes or for the possibility of the opposition getting the ball and kicking it downfield.

The full-back is also the ideal person to counter-attack, as so many stray kicks go to him. This provides the opportunity for many different plays. He can combine with either of his own wings by direct passing, scissors or dummy scissors. He can go on his own by sidestepping or by 'running through' an opponent. Another move is to put in a high kick with the idea of either tackling the catcher in possession or making ground to where the ball lands, jumping and winning the ball. There is tremendous variety.

Handling is one of the most important arts of back play. Most players think passing the ball is just throwing it backwards to the next player. It is much more than this, it is passing *accurately* so that the next player takes the ball out in front of his body with his hands and *not* against his body. It is amazing how much faster the ball moves along a three-quarter line by this method than if every pass is into the player's body. Finger-tip passing is the best and the correct method of moving the ball at speed.

The main intention of the midfield backs is to cross the gain line. This is an imaginary line which passes between the two teams – from a scrum, for instance, it passes down the tunnel across the field. This applies in the same way from line-outs, mauls and rucks. Even if you get only one inch over the gain line, it still means that your side is attacking. The same idea applies in scrummaging: if your pack pushes the opposing pack back one inch the whole side are attacking.

Most sides have one player in the back division who calls the moves, and obviously these depend on the situation of the game. It is difficult for the full-back to call the moves, as he is so far away from the rest of the backs there is difficulty in communicating, especially when there are large, noisy crowds. So if the full-back is calling a 'set-piece' situation he must move up and make himself heard.

Defence of the whole back line is vital. The system I have always used in marking opposing three-quarters lines is that my wing always stays with his man, while those inside take the man with the ball. This might mean the opposing side making a break, but if the wing is marked by his opposite man it is far easier for the back row and full-back to stop the man with the ball. This is called 'isolating the man in possession'. Also, if the opposition kicked, the whole three-quarter line must be prepared to turn round and get back quickly to support the man who fields the ball, whether he be full-back, wing or centre. This applies to kicks of any kind, even goal kicks which fail to find the target.

Effective kicking is achieved when your side regains possession from, say, a high kick to the posts, where the centre jumps and catches the ball either to run on or to create a winning maul situation. It is essential when kicking not to give the ball straight back to your opponents. If the backs have to kick, which is almost an absolute necessity when going backwards, then it must be constructive, offering a fair chance of regaining possession, winning valuable ground or giving the opposition poor ball.

Examples of kicking put to good use are:

(1) kicking the ball dead from a kick-off
(2) kicking high to the post
(3) kicking 'into the box', the blind side space between opposition wing and full-back
(4) making a long rolling kick to the far wing, so stretching the opposing full-back
(5) quick drop-outs from the 25 yd line
(6) kicking 'the wrong way' from a kick-off, i.e. fooling the opposition you are going to kick left for the forwards, and then another player kicking to the right for the wing.

Penalty kicks are a very important aspect of the game. If it is a short penalty situation the scrum-half must act by moving the ball straight away. If the captain wants something else, like a kick to touch or at goal, then he must shout quickly to stop the scrum-half. One great advantage of a short penalty is its speed and its element of surprise. Very often, too, the opposition fail to retire the necessary ten yards, and you gain another ten yards for a further penalty – this time possibly within range of goal.

This raises the question of who should be the goal kicker in the team. In the past the full-back was usually the goal-kicker. Now that every player is picked for his team because he is the best specialist in a particular position, the best goal kicker takes the kicks. If there is no goal kicker in the side one must be brought in, for however much one dislikes the idea goal kickers win or lose matches. However, it is unusual if in fifteen international-class players there is no one who can put the ball between the posts. Fly-halves seem to be the commonest goal kickers nowadays, to judge by Phil Bennett and Alan Old in South Africa and Barry John in New Zealand.

The last Test in South Africa was an example of the cost of goal kicks being missed. In the first half Jackie Snyman had about four kicks for the Springboks from the 25 line, and all of them went astray. Then, with the Lions 10–6 up at the start of the second half, we had two chances at goal which would have put us in probably an unassailable position of 16–6. Alas, both kicks missed their target, the Springboks were still in striking distance, and we had to settle for a draw.

The quick drop-out is very useful, as the ball can be thrown to an unmarked player, who just taps it over the line and sets off an attack from his own 25. This happened in the Lions–Transvaal game, when a short drop-out enabled Dick Milliken to make his way into the Transvaal 25. Unfortunately the try that should have been achieved did not materialise, but sixty valuable yards had been gained by quick thinking, all due to each member of the team concentrating.

Here, briefly, are some of the three-quarter moves that have been used in Britain and by the Lions over the past five years:

(1) MISS MOVE – this entails missing out one player in a movement. For example, if the inside centre is left out the ball is passed from the fly-half to the outside centre, usually with the full-back coming in between the outside centre and the wing. The full-back can alternate his line of entry and other players can be excluded.

(2) RANGI – this entails a scissors between either (a) fly-half and outside centre or (b) inside centre and wing. This move was named after the Maori All Black centre, Ron Rangi.

(3) SCISSORS between the two centres.

(4) DUMMY CRASH – dummy scissors between two centres with the full-back taking the ball on the burst from a flat pass.

(5) Blind side wing taking the ball from the fly-half, either outside or inside.

(6) Open side wing taking ball from inside centre, with outside centre running wide.

(7) LOOP – fly-half passes to inside centre then runs around and collects the ball on the outside.

(8) DUMMY LOOP – same as loop, except inside centre does not give ball to fly-half but passes to player coming on the inside.

These are only a few examples of the moves which can be developed. However, it is far better to have only three or four well prepared moves than ten that are poorly developed. If they are carried out properly it is very difficult for the opposition to do much about it, and there should be alternatives if it seems the opposition have 'cottoned on'. This, of course, is where the experience of a player comes in.

The important deficiencies in South Africa and New Zealand back play were in their basic skills. If things are going wrong put the basics right and you're half way there.

HANDLING is vital. A glaring example of bad handling was shown in the fourth Test at Ellis Park when Jackie Snyman made a lovely break for South Africa and came through to me with Gert Muller outside him. I was committed to tackling Snyman and thought a try was inevitable. To my delight a perfect scoring pass was knocked on by Muller and a chance of a winning score lost – a prime example of handling deficiency.

OVERLAP: At times, even when facing an overlap situation, say four men to our three, the Lions were able to make opponents pass without tackling them, thus shuttling them across the field and eventually into touch. Here again the opposition had overlooked the principle of drawing a man before passing.

TACKLING: This is probably the most important facet of back play, but was certainly lacking in the Springboks' second Test side at Pretoria. Their tackling was so weak that at times the Lions were under the impression they were playing touch-rugby. You can turn defence into attack with a really hard tackle, allowing the loose ball to be driven through.

COUNTER-ATTACKING features prominently in the British Isles, but it seems not to exist in South Africa or New Zealand. Since the change of the new touch-kicking laws the opportunity to run the ball back at the opposition has been greatly increased.

I believe many shortcomings in basic skills could be put right with correct coaching at an early age. However, coaching if overdone can be destructive. New Zealand were so obsessed with the 'MacRae' type of centre three-quarter play that any kid trying to show any sort of individualism was told: 'Don't try to sidestep in New Zealand, just run straight.' This is bad coaching, because it stifles flair, and it is one of the reasons why very few players in New Zealand or South Africa can sidestep. It is more difficult to understand in South Africa, as the hard dry grounds are ideally suited to this sort of play rather than running straight into an opponent and being tackled.

FIELDING: Catching the high ball is one of the basics of full-back play. The eye should be kept on the ball at all times and in no circumstances must the full-back look at the opposition bearing down on him. The catcher should stand with his side turned to the opposition, or alternatively front on, but should remember to turn sideways when catching the ball. His arms should be extended, making a 'cradle' to receive the ball. In no circumstances should the ball be caught just with the hands – it is the *arms* which collect the ball. At the moment of impact there is some 'give' of the arms.

It is crucial to turn sideways on catching the ball, as this is self-preservation against the oncoming players. In certain circumstances it may be necessary to raise the nearer knee, or to stick an elbow out to discourage players keen on the dangerous habit of late tackling. A full-back lays himself open by standing front forwards; the shoulders and back are far more resistant to injuries. Turning on receiving the ball has been of immense value to me and has contributed in no little way to my relative freedom from injury. The best example of this was the Lions–New Zealand third Test in 1971 at Wellington, which I mentioned earlier. Had I not turned my back I doubt very much whether I would have stayed on the field and seen the game out.

TACKLING: A full-back usually has to pull off the most difficult tackle of all – the head-on encounter. To do this requires courage, timing, a good push-off when going into the tackle, strong shoulders and arms and the need to get your head to the side. The situation is much more desperate if the full-back is near his own goal-line – a 'pure' tackle will not prevent the opponent falling over the line and scoring. In these circumstances the full-back must 'smother' the opponent by grabbing his chest, with the ball between them, and attempting to force him backwards. This, obviously, is difficult to achieve, but when done well is very satisfying.

MY OWN MEMORIES OF 'LAST LINE' TACKLES

(1) Lions–North Auckland, 1971. There was a triple scissors between the three Going brothers, which led to Sid Going coming towards me with fifteen yards to the line for what could have been the winning try. I stopped him dead, and so saved the situation.

(2) Lions–South Africa, fourth Test, 1974. Chris Pope was away on the wing for South Africa. He fended off J. J. Williams and had just myself to beat. I went in low (he is $14\frac{1}{2}$ stone) and brought him down over the touchline. Unfortunately Pope managed to fling the ball infield and the Springboks scored a controversial try (their only try against the Lions) but my job had been done well.

(3) Wales–the President's XV, 1970. David Duckham

was put away on the half way line and had only me to beat. I 'read' his sidestep and took him, with our defence otherwise completely broken.

When tackling I always try to 'psyche out' my opponent. I keep my eyes on him and try to stare him out. In this way he is watching me and can in some cases become 'mesmerised'. Then, as he is thinking what to do, I move forward, catching him by surprise. This is particularly useful against a player with a good sidestep. Theoretically if they have room to move in they should always beat a full-back. The full-back's job is to prove the theory wrong.

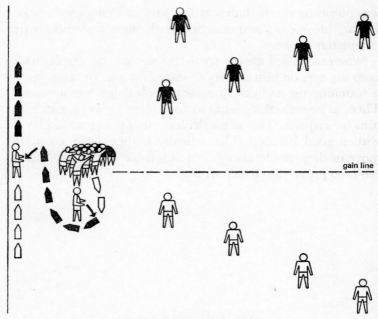

gain line

BACK ROW PLOYS

A key factor to any move worked by the back row forwards is effective scrummaging. It is preferable if the opposition is forced to retreat, putting their own back row under pressure. Well channelled and quick ball is also important. Obviously the type of moves used depends on the talent available and the quality of the opposition. It is useless to use flankers off the scrum unless they are exceptionally fast. Most back row ploys are used going right as obviously it is easier for the scrum-half to break this side and feed a back row forward or accept a pass from, say, the No. 8.

This diagram, however, illustrates a different ploy. The right hand flanker withdraws from the back of the scrum as the ball is won, and after receiving a pass from the scrum-half he drives forward supported by the left wing on the outside and No. 8 plus scrum-half inside. This move can also take place on the open side when the flanker can then link directly with his backs.

There are many variations to this ploy, and a little thought can devise what is best suited to your unit. The 1974 Lions often used the No. 8 to pick up and take advantage of Gareth Edwards's or John Moloney's speed at scrum-half; alternatively the No. 8 can pass first to a flanker with the scrum-half in support; the scrum-half can break directly himself going a little wide, and be supported on the outside by the full-back and blind side wing.

Note: The Gain Line is the line running at right angles to touch through scrum, line-out, ruck or maul. The Tackle line is the line that runs mid way between the feet of the two opposing back lines.

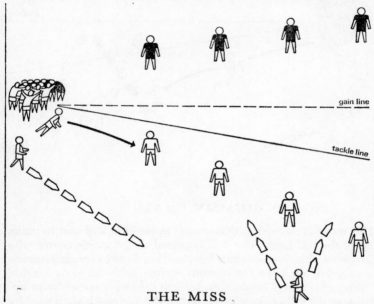

THE MISS

When attacking from a set piece one of the most effective methods of stretching the opposing defence is to miss out one of your own backs and bring the full-back into the line. In this diagram the full-back joins the line either between the centres or between the outside centre and the wing. If the F.B. enters between the centres he automatically straightens the line of attack and passes direct to the outside wing missing out the outside centre. If he enters on the alternative line the inside centre is missed out as the opposite centres will be automatically drawn.

When the full-back joins his three-quarters the blind side wing (in this case on the left) covers his position in case of a breakdown. This wing can also join the attack to make an extra man by linking and taking the scrum-half's pass or moving up outside the fly-half.

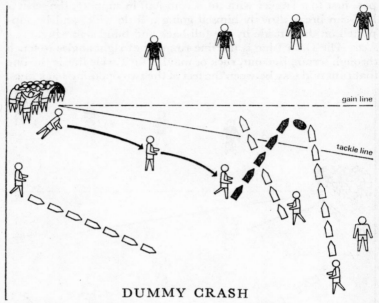

gain line

tackle line

DUMMY CRASH

This move is devised to deceive the opposition and also to make use of the full-back. The ball is passed to the inside centre who runs across his three-quarter line, making for the opposing outside centre. He then does a dummy switch with his own outside centre, who moves inside him. Instead the inside centre 'pops up' a pass to the full-back, who has joined the line and is supported by the right wing. The opposing centres will have been forced to mark their opposite numbers. It is important for the attacking line to lie well back to provide plenty of room for the movement. Otherwise they might knock the ball on through lack of space.

An alternative move is called the 'Rangi', after the former All Blacks centre. Here the fly-half receives the ball and runs across to the opposite outside centre. His own inside centre goes with him as if to receive the ball. Instead the outside centre comes in from behind and receives a switch pass. He should run as straight as possible. Ideally a gap will appear in the defence, but even if caught he is likely to have broken the advantage line and will be able to create a situation for good second-phase possession.

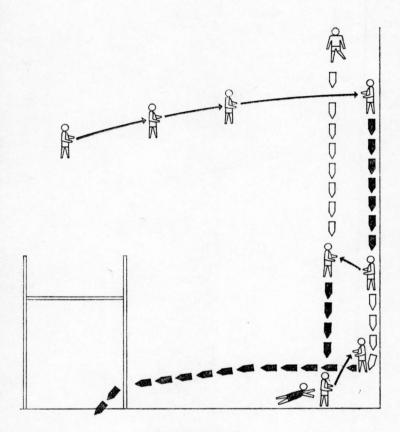

MISS J. P. R.

This move was used successfully in the third Test against South Africa in Port Elizabeth when the Lions won the series. The ball was won from the line-out and Williams moved up outside his centres but was deliberately missed out of the passing move, leaving wing J. J. Williams to streak down the touchline with the Springboks wondering why the ball had not been passed to J. P. R. As J. J. Williams drew the full-back he passed inside to J. P. R., who hoped to cross the line, but when about to be tackled by the cover defence he turned and returned the ball to J. J., who went on to score between the posts.

Part Three

THE OPPOSITION
SPEAKS

The Lions in New Zealand

COLIN MEADS

If I were to relate the performances of the 1971 Lions in New Zealand with others of those composite British Isles teams against whom I played I could not do better than to repeat what I said to those Lions: 'You are the greatest touring team I have played against. You are great because you have stopped believing in fairy tales.' That judgment was received with comment good and bad yet it was not made without thought, nor do I believe it to be an over-simplification. Through the Lions of 1971 and the men who inspired them British rugby became adult – in the sense that the team and those who supported them realised that Test matches are to be won, and that it is difficult to win them without realistic planning. To achieve success there had to be a new mental and physical attitude to the business of winning parity, at least in that area of rugby where matches are won, always have been and ever will be: in the forwards, in those pieces of play from which possession is won. It was in this that the 1971 Lions succeeded most dramatically.

When all the praise – and it is justified – has been given to men like Carwyn James and Ray McLoughlin and Dougie Smith we must come again to the essential ingredient, the players of the game. I do not except Ray McLoughlin from them but it was in the planning and technical sense that Ray had such an influence on the players. The injury which disqualified him from participation in the Tests was, in an ironic way, one of the reasons why they won the series, because he concentrated his attention, almost fanatically, on the techniques he knew the Lions must perfect to win.

Where the Lions of 1959 and 1966 set out to attack, they did so too often from positions which were not controlled, from positions where the opposition was not committed and, therefore, where the defences were set and in depth. There were fine players in these teams, but the conception of what had to be achieved before they could express their talents was not of the same standard. The 1971 team had players of brilliance in the backs and they were given their head in many of the provincial matches. But when it came to the tests the head ruled the heart, and these Lions played the sort of utilitarian rugby which, allied with magnificent defence and stout forward play, is terribly difficult to beat.

I can imagine the ecstasy with which such players as David Hewitt, Peter Jackson, Malcolm Price, the Mike Gibson of 1966 and others would have regarded the capacity of the forwards to clench and hold or drive, to win possession going forward instead of allowing it to dribble back with everyone immediately placed under pressure, to play with discipline and control.

If I have a qualification about the development of this new spirit it would be that, having achieved the techniques to scrum with the best, to contest possession from all sources, British rugby should not allow itself to become top-heavy. It appears in danger of doing so. By that I mean that Britain should not now cut its backs out of the game. The new forward power and skill should have given the British the platform from which – with devastating effectiveness – they can play total rugby better than any other nation in the world. It would be a great pity were traditional brilliance in one area of the game now to be squandered because Britain has found such quality in another.

It seemed to me, too, that for the first time in my experience the Lions were able to weld nationally. Previous teams obviously suffered from internal pressures and disruptions resulting from the inability of players and management to recognise that theirs was a British team, and not a motley collection of a few Scots, a few English, a few Irish and a few Welsh. They lacked the true *team* philosophy, and they suffered for it. There was never any evidence of this off the field in 1971, nor any manifestation of it in their team selections or attitudes on the field.

My first experience with the Lions was in 1959 when as a reserve at Carisbrook, Dunedin, I watched Don Clarke kick six penalty goals to give New Zealand an 18–17 victory against a Lions team which scored four tries. That sort of defeat would upset me, too. Yet with the laws as they were then the referee was right, and scoring tries was not necessarily enough to win a game against a team kicking penalty goals. My observation that day was that the Lions had only themselves to blame for losing what could so easily and deservedly have been a slashing victory. I am aware that though they were beaten in the series the Lions of 1959 believed deeply they were the better team. The same story could have been true in 1971. I believe New Zealand, with constant goal-kicking, would have beaten the Lions. But this is all hypothetical. The facts of wins and losses are straightforward enough.

The year 1971 saw the great awakening of British rugby. For years they had watched their teams being beaten by All Blacks who used their possession with stiff-necked utilitarianism, who spread their wings only rarely – and then when it seemed it was safe to do so from positions of control. While the All Blacks were doing this, the Lions, receiving much less controlled possession, and often as they were moving back, or without the New Zealanders having committed themselves, would launch uninhibited attacks which were doomed before they started. In 1971 the roles were reversed. The British and, I suspect, Carwyn James in particular, had worked out their priorities and had decided that there was a great deal to be said for winning – even in the game of rugger. They went about their transition with expertise and dedication. Some of their training sessions in New Zealand were mind-boggling as they 'pretended' to practise line-outs the so-called New Zealand way. They obstructed in about every conceivable way, laughed it off and then went out into their matches – and did exactly the same thing. Heaven forbid that

I should condemn them for it: I've been known on odd occasions to indulge in minor matters of obstruction myself! I offer it simply as an illustration of how far the 1971 Lions were prepared – and able – to go in pursuit of their Test victory.

It has become accepted by New Zealand players that it was harder to beat a Welsh pack at Cardiff Arms, a Scottish pack at Murrayfield, an Irish pack at Lansdowne Road, or, yes, an English pack at Twickenham, than it was to beat the cream of all of them whipped into a composite scrum on tour. Even when we beat England 14–0 at Twickenham in 1963–64 the English pack held us and more in the second spell. We always had a battle with the Welsh club packs and the Borderers at Hawick or the men of Munster; but try to tie them up into a British pack and they lacked this abrasive national spirit, lacked, it seemed at times, even the will to work together with efficiency.

The 1971 Lions changed all that, and not only through their willingness to tie themselves into a multi-national knot. It was through a fine application of technical know-how. It was not funny being in the middle of a New Zealand pack which was going backward. Occasionally you went backward against the Springboks – but, my God, never against the Lions!

There were good players in Mike Campbell-Lamerton's 1966 team, but they lacked motivation and they lacked, I regret to say, the will to put aside considerations other than those of playing rugby with their hearts and souls. Campbell-Lamerton had my respect as a man and my sympathy as a captain even though at times he may have made odd decisions. But I never saw him do other than strive for his team when he was on the paddock. Could all those 1966 Lions truly say the same? While recognising that there were frustrations on that tour I would point out, too, that there are frustrations on every tour but you seek to overcome them. A comparison of the 1966 Lions and the 1971 Lions would be oversimplified by saying that one team had a deep, burning compulsion to do well – no, to *win* – while the other was riven with discontent, wandering about with a total lack of direction. Yet it would be fair to point also to the different states of New Zealand rugby. In 1966 the All Blacks were in the middle of as fine an era of rugby as this country has had. The pack was full of thinking players – six of them captains of their provinces. In comparison the 1971 pack was a learning pack, still raw to the ways of international rugby yet in some facets of the game still able to take over from what was then the finest pack the British had fielded in their rugby history. It was the Lions' great fortune that they found New Zealand rugby in a transitional stage, but that is an issue beyond the main theorem – the QED of which is that intelligent planning based on dedicated and even inspired players in key positions equals success in rugby tests.

The 1971 team had us licked in an area of possession-winning, the area in which New Zealand had always been strong and from which many of the All Blacks' most pungent attacking episodes through the years had stemmed. This was at the back of the line-out. Here Mervyn Davies had us donkey-licked. In fact, were I asked to nominate two players who, beyond all others, contributed most to the defeat of the All Blacks in that series I would name Davies and Mike Gibson. Each in his own way hurt the All Black cause alarmingly. It was not just that Davies achieved domination for the Lions at the back of the line-out. He moved with quite startling speed and intelligence – an instinctive reaction almost – to trouble-spots, killing ball till the Lions could regroup.

Gibson was as near to the perfect rugby player as I have seen in any position. We knew what a fine attacking player he was, whether in the centres or at fly-half, from having played against him when he was at Cambridge on the '63–'64 tour, and from what he was able to make of the comparative crumbs the Lions of '66 offered him. But in 1971 his rugby was comprehensively magnificent. I shudder at the recollection of how many New Zealand attacks, well considered, well constructed, foundered upon Mike Gibson. He was the real king of these Lions – and I say that with great respect to Barry John. Gibson covered every uncertainty or error of John and I would judge that eighty per cent – yes, eighty per cent – of the New Zealand back movements came unstuck through Gibson's quickness, skill and courage.

Yes, the Lions of 1971 stopped believing in those old fairy tales. But I wonder whether another fairy tale is not already born – that because you have developed strength forward then, *ipso facto*, you can forget your old strengths. That could be as damaging to British rugby in the long run as the proposition that you can muck about with poor forward play as long as you have brilliant backs. I see Britain as being in a unique position in world rugby, but I wonder if the British themselves appreciate it. New strength in the forwards has not automatically cancelled out brilliance in the backs. So why not use the new to exploit the traditional? That seems to make a lot of rugby sense to me.

The South African Tour

HANNES MARAIS

To make comparisons is always an odious task, mainly because of the many variable factors involved, but during the period from 1963 in which I wore the Springbok jersey I cannot recall playing against a better team than Willie John McBride's 1974 British Lions. They were superior, for instance, to Brian Lochore's 1970 All Blacks, another of the great modern teams, though the 1970 All Blacks were a very fine team indeed, and it was a remarkable achievement on our part to have beaten them.

Much of the blame for the 1970 All Blacks' failure in South Africa was laid at the door of their tour selectors, but their biggest mistake – and the major difference between them and the 1974 Lions – was their total predictability. 'The pattern,' which during the late '60s had been one of the most significant props of their invincibility, was their undoing. They were so obsessed with second-phase rugby they neglected the vital first phase. Johan Claassen, our coach, spotted this and under his direction we based our entire strategy on breaking their pattern by stopping them from coming over the advantage line. I doubt whether the All Blacks ever really cottoned on to what was happening, and for that reason they were not able to read our game as clearly as we could read theirs.

The 1974 Lions were completely different. They played copybook football when it came to basics, but they had no set pattern, and while we always knew what they were up to they were so flexible and yet so well drilled and efficient there was very little we could do about it. At least, not with the team we fielded. How did the Lions compare with the French teams I have played against? Well, there are no better handlers of the ball than the French – and woe betide you if you happen to strike them on one of their on-days! But generally none of the modern French teams would come near to matching the discipline and organisation of the Lions, and for this reason I doubt whether any of them could have beaten McBride and his men.

However, I do not want to give the impression that the greatness of the 1974 Lions was based solely on their exceptional cohesion and organisation. They also had a host of individuals of star quality.

Gareth Edwards, their general and on-the-field strategist-in-chief, has never played better rugby in his life. Certainly I have never played against a better scrum-half in a test match. His kicking punished us severely, while his long passes made it extremely difficult to get anywhere near Phil Bennett – whom we always considered as the one possible weak link in the Lions team. And Edwards's break was not only a constant worry to our loose forwards but was responsible for setting up some crucial tries. If I had a criticism of Edwards it was the way he constantly baited the referees. That they allowed it to happen does not in any way condone his behaviour, which was against the spirit of the game and unbecoming of a player of his calibre.

J. P. R. Williams is another of the Lions whom I would list in my teams of the best-ever opponents. He was like the rock of Gibraltar to the Lions. We were never able to pressurise him as we would have liked, and even when we did his defence was impeccable. I finished the series with a particularly high regard for his physical and mental toughness. We grassed him severely at times, and raked him, too, but he always came back more aggressive than before.

I would not rate any of the other Lions back line so highly, yet they did mould themselves into an extremely efficient and thrustful force before the tour was over. They were fortunate, to be sure, to be playing behind a pack that gave them so much good possession, and they were superbly protected by Edwards and Bennett, who seldom put them under pressure. When they did get the ball they used it so wisely and

so well that they never made the kind of mistakes that forag-
ers like Jan Ellis and Morne du Plessis could use to our
advantage. Dick Milliken grew in stature with every Test,
Andy Irvine proved to be a footballer of exceptional talent,
but of all the three-quarters J. J. Williams was the pick. His
exceptional speed brought him four Test tries and his thirst
for work made him a constant scourge.

Up front the Lions' pack were the finest I have ever played
against in the Test arena. Their front row trio of McLauchlan, Windsor and Cotton were all admirably equipped for
their roles, but I hesitate to name them as the best front row
I have ever packed against as they had behind them what
was the best organised shove I have ever opposed. The 1974
Lions were the most effective scrummagers to tour this
country – and for the last fifty years or so we have been the
masters of the tight scrum, and because of it masters of the
world. I have, it is true, always regarded the British as good
scrummagers – better than the All Blacks, French or
Australians – but they never before have produced anything
like this. They obviously came to South Africa with the
belief that scrummaging superiority was the key to victory.
To scrum as they scrummed is a fine art that takes a lot of
thought, work and experience. Their advances in technical
skill came as a shock at the start of the series and we only
came up with some answers in the final Test. The Lions
mastered the techniques of scrummaging so well that, when
Edwards put the ball in, they were able to hold the scrum
steady and feed him the ball whenever he asked for it. When
we put the ball in they would produce a massive hip shove a
split second after we had heeled – and so were off balance –
and the strike would become bad ball and practically
useless.

At the line-outs the Lions were sound, but no more than
that. In fact, in our own John Williams we had a trump card,
and it was a grave mistake to have dropped him for the third
Test at Port Elizabeth. The Lions' rucking and mauling
techniques were also good. They drove in well, they hunted

together and their technique was sound, but, as with the line-outs, they were unable to overwhelm us as they did at the tight scrums.

McBride's men were also well organised for back row attacks, but while we feared this aspect of their play we were well prepared for it. Though they were a menace to some of our provincial sides, they never troubled us unduly in the Tests. The one exception was Fergus Slattery who, given much more freedom than our own committed loose forwards, created havoc among our backs.

Each one of the Lions' forwards filled their role so well I find it difficult to single any one of them out, but if I must McLauchlan was probably their most valuable forward. He seemed to be the brains behind their scrummaging technique. He also seemed to be the pack leader on the field. I know McBride was the captain, but on the field it was 'Mighty Mouse' who seemed to do all the talking. I only really heard McBride giving orders in the final Test, when things began to go wrong for his team. He got agitated – too agitated, I thought – and some hard words were barked at his men. Nevertheless I have immense respect for McBride as a captain. I find his approach to rugby and sport most acceptable, and any man who can command the loyalty that he did has to be an exceptional leader.

I would also like to record two criticisms of the Lions. The first is that we found them extremely unsociable. At the start of the tour, after the match against Eastern Province, Syd Millar approached me with a special request. He said that the 1968 Lions had found the Springboks cold and unfriendly and suggested that we work together to remedy the problem. I agreed, and so did Johan Claassen when I mentioned Syd's request to him. The upshot was that we were at great pains during the series to get to the various receptions on time and try to mix with the Lions. Unfortunately we were given a cold shoulder. There were some notable exceptions, none more so than the ever-friendly 'Mighty Mouse' and Syd himself, but generally speaking we found the Lions too busy to have any time to join with us. Here I must include even Willie John.

I have made this point specifically because of the frequent accusations that have been made of Springbok teams in the past. Even Syd's approach to me in Port Elizabeth was an accusation in a way. Has unsociability got something to do with dedication? Was it all part of the new approach of the breed of winners being reared in British rugby? Was their indifference something born of a superiority complex? I cannot answer these questions, but I think it is something the Lions might bear in mind. It might help them to understand the past and improve their image in the future.

My second criticism concerns the Lions' gamesmanship. This impregnated their game to a degree that was not only unnecessary but which might be damaging to British rugby in the future. They played as far outside the laws as possible, especially when it came to putting the ball in the scrum and to obstruction. They got away with it in South Africa, but they will not always do so. And when they are no longer allowed this freedom their game is going to suffer.

Dr Danie Craven made it clear during the Springbok tour of France, which followed close on the heels of the Lions' visit to South Africa, that in future neutral referees would be asked to cover all international matches in South Africa. That is some of the best news I have heard in a long time. I would be less than honest if I did not say that we were unhappy with the South African referees who handled the four Tests. It might sound like sour grapes, but in most cases the benefit of the doubt went to the Lions, partly, I think, because the referees were victims of a system which put them under unhealthy pressure. There is another point which I feel should be stressed. It has been my experience in the past that when a touring team has been unhappy with local referees the referees of their country have invariably taken it out on the Springboks on subsequent tours. This is totally wrong. A referee should stand or fall as an individual; an entire country should not have to suffer for his sins. With 'neutral' or independent referees this should not happen again.

Having attempted to put the 1974 Lions team into perspective I want to say it was unfortunate that we played them when we did. We simply were not geared to take on such formidable opponents, but South African rugby was not so much in the doldrums as many people believed. There was nothing seriously wrong with our style or play, though there were areas which needed to be improved. Our major problem was that we did not have a chance to build an international team. Most of the stalwarts of the '60s and early '70s had departed, and without an international tour since 1971, and only one home Test in the two years after that, we were forced to use the series for experiment. Tours are vital for survival as a world rugby power. Without them it is difficult to rebuild when retirements and injuries take their toll. Mistakes were made in 1974 and there were disasters – like the second Test at Loftus Versfelt – but they helped us to find our feet. On the strength of our draw in the final Test and our victories later in France I am convinced that it would be very different if we had played the Lions again in 1975.

I do not subscribe to the theory that the advantage during a Test series is always with the touring team. An established home team playing in season should have the upper hand. When a team is rebuilding, it is quite different. Tours can help to work minor miracles – to build spirit, understanding and morale. They also pin-point the players with that all-important big-match temperament. And the atmosphere can often turn a hitherto average player into an outstanding one.

Appendices

THE LIONS' RECORD

1. Lions Tour of New Zealand 1971[1]

May 22nd   BEAT THAMES VALLEY COUNTIES (Pukekohe)
                                                             25–3

Thames Valley   Pen goal: McCallum.
Counties:

Lions: Tries: Taylor, Edwards, Spencer; con: John (2); pen goals: John (3); drop goal: John.

May 26th   BEAT WANGANUI–KING COUNTRY (Wanganui)
                                                             22–9

Wanganui–King   Tries: Milburn, Virtue; pen goal: Rush.
Country:

Lions: Tries: Mervyn Davies, Bevan (2); con: Hiller (2); pen goals: Hiller (3).

May 29th   BEAT WAIKATO (Hamilton)   35–14

Waikato: Try: Skudder; con: Pickrang; pen goals: Pickrang (2); drop goal: Pickrang.

Lions: Tries: Bevan (3), Dawes, Quinnell, McLoughlin, John; con: Hiller (3), John; pen goal: John; drop goal: John.

June 2nd   BEAT NEW ZEALAND MAORIS (Auckland)   23–12

New Zealand Maoris: Pen goals: Pickrang (4).
Lions: Try: Bevan; con: John; pen goals: John (6)

June 5th   BEAT WELLINGTON (Wellington)   47–9

Wellington: Pen goals: Gregg (2); drop goal: Dougan.
Lions: Tries: Bevan (4), Gibson (2), Carmichael, Taylor, John; con: John (5), Gibson, Williams; pen goals: John (2).

[1] During the 1971 tour tries were still only worth three points. By 1974 they were worth four.

June 9th   BEAT SOUTH CANTERBURY–MID   25–6
                  CANTERBURY–NORTH OTAGO

South Canterbury–Mid   Pen goals: Twaddell (2).
  Canterbury–North
  Otago:
Lions: Tries: Gerald Davies (2), Duckham, Rea,
                  Hopkins; con: Hiller (2); pen goals:
                  Hiller (2).

June 12th   BEAT OTAGO (Dunedin)   21–9
Otago: Try: Collins; con: L. W. Mains; pen goal:
                  Mains.
Lions: Tries: Taylor, Williams, Dawes; con:
                  John (3); pen goal: John; drop goal:
                  John.

June 16th   BEAT WEST COAST–BULLER   39–6
                  (Greymouth)
West Coast–Buller: Try: Stewart; pen goal: Hart.
Lions: Tries: Duckham (6), Biggar, Hiller; con:
                  Hiller (6); pen goal: Hiller.

June 19th   BEAT CANTERBURY (Christchurch)   14–3
Canterbury: Pen goal: McCormick.
Lions: Tries: Bevan, Lewis; con: Williams; pen
                  goals: Gibson, Williams.

June 22nd   BEAT MARLBOROUGH–NELSON BAYS (Blenheim)
                                     31–12
Marlborough–Nelson   Tries: Allan, Ray Sutherland, Gleeson,
  Bays: Alan Sutherland.
Lions: Tries: Biggar (3), Gibson, Dixon, Gerald
                  Davies, Rea; con: Hiller (5).

June 26th   BEAT NEW ZEALAND (Dunedin)   9–3
New Zealand: Pen goal: McCormick.
Lions: Try: McLauchlan; pen goals: John (2).

June 30th   BEAT SOUTHLAND (Invercargill)   25–3

Southland: Pen goal: Nicol.

Lions: Tries: Biggar (2), Taylor, Dawes, Mervyn Davies; con: John (5).

July 3rd   BEAT TARANAKI (New Plymouth)   14–9

Taranaki: Tries: Hill, Vesty; pen goal: Hill.

Lions: Try: Mervyn Davies; con: Hiller; pen goal: Hiller; drop goals: Hiller, Gibson.

July 6th   BEAT NEW ZEALAND UNIVERSITIES   27–6 (Wellington)

New Zealand Universities: Tries: Collins (2).

Lions: Tries: John, Duckham, Bevan; con: John (3); pen goals: John (3); drop goal: John.

July 10th   LOST NEW ZEALAND (Christchurch)   12–22

New Zealand: Tries: Burgess (2), Going, I. A. Kirkpatrick; pen try; con: L. W. Mains (2); pen goal: Mains.

Lions: Tries: Gerald Davis (2); pen goal: John; drop goal: John.

July 14th   BEAT WAIRARAPA–BUSH (Masterton)   27–6

Wairarapa–Bush: Try: Couch; pen goal: Marfell.

Lions: Tries: John (2), Biggar (2), Spencer, Edwards; con: John (2), Hiller.

July 17th   BEAT HAWKES BAY (Napier)   25–6

Hawkes Bay: Pen goal: Bishop; drop goal: Thornton.

Lions: Tries: Gerald Davies (4); con: John (2); pen goals: John (2); drop goal: John.

July 21st   BEAT POVERTY BAY–EAST COAST   18–12
             (Gisborne)

Poverty Bay–East   Try: Ussher; pen goals: Mabey (3).
   Coast:
Lions: Tries: Duckham (2), Edwards; pen goals:
                          Hiller (2); drop goal: Dawes.

July 24th   BEAT AUCKLAND (Auckland)   19–12
Auckland: Pen goals: R. G. Whatman (2), B. G.
                          Williams; drop goal: Whatman.
Lions: Tries: Evans, Dawes; con: John (2); pen
                          goal: John (3).

July 31st   BEAT NEW ZEALAND (Wellington)   13–3
New Zealand: Try: Mains.
Lions: Tries: Gerald Davies, John; con: John
                          (2); drop goal: John.

August 4th   BEAT MANAWATU–HOROWHENUA   39–6
             (Palmerston North)
Manawatu–   Pen goal: Karam; drop goal: Karam.
   Horowhenua:
Lions: Tries: Bevan (4), Lewis, Spencer, Gibson,
                          Hiller; con: Hiller (3); pen goals: Hiller
                          (3).

August 7th   BEAT NORTH AUCKLAND (Whangarei)   11–5
North Auckland: Try: Guy; con: Going.
Lions: Tries: Duckham, Williams, Bevan; con:
                          John.

August 10th BEAT BAY OF PLENTY (Tauranga)   20–14
Bay of Plenty: Tries: G. Moore, B. Trask, R. Walker;
                          con: Trask; pen goal: Trask.
Lions: Tries: Biggar, Gibson; con: Hiller; pen
                          goals: Hiller (3); drop goal: John.

August 14th   DREW NEW ZEALAND (Auckland)   14–14
New Zealand: Tries: Cottrell, T. N. Lister; con: L. W.
                         Mains; pen goals: Mains (2).
Lions: Try: Dixon; con: John; pen goals: John
                         (2); drop goal: Williams.

N.B.   The Lions played two matches in Australia before arriving
in New Zealand. They lost the first 11–15 to Queensland (Brisbane) and beat New South Wales (Sydney) 14–12.

PLAYER		A	T	C	PG	DG	PTS
BARRY JOHN	(Wales)	16	6	30	26	8	180
BOB HILLER	(England)	10	2	24	14	2	102
JOHN BEVAN	(Wales)	13	17	—	—	—	51
DAVID DUCKHAM	(England)	15[1]	11	—	—	—	33
GERALD DAVIES	(Wales)	10	10	—	—	—	30
ALISTAIR BIGGAR	(Scotland)	9	9	—	—	—	27
MIKE GIBSON	(Ireland)	15	5	1	1	1	23
J. P. R. WILLIAMS	(Wales)	14	2	2	1	1	16
JOHN DAWES	(Wales)	17	4	—	—	1	15
JOHN TAYLOR	(Wales)	14	4	—	—	—	12
JOHN SPENCER	(England)	9	3	—	—	—	9
GARETH EDWARDS	(Wales)	15	3	—	—	—	9
MERVYN DAVIES	(Wales)	13	3	—	—	—	9
CHRIS REA	(Scotland)	10[1]	3	—	—	—	9
PETER DIXON	(England)	14	2	—	—	—	6
ARTHUR LEWIS	(Wales)	8	2	—	—	—	6
IAN MCLAUCHLAN	(Scotland)	15	1	—	—	—	3
RAY HOPKINS	(Wales)	10[1]	1	—	—	—	3
DEREK QUINNELL	(Wales)	9	1	—	—	—	3
GEOFF EVANS	(Wales)	6	1	—	—	—	3
SANDY CARMICHAEL	(Scotland)	5	1	—	—	—	3
RAY MCLOUGHLIN	(Ireland)	5	1	—	—	—	3
JOHN PULLIN	(England)	15	—	—	—	—	0
WILLIE JOHN MCBRIDE	(Ireland)	14[1]	—	—	—	—	0
SEAN LYNCH	(Ireland)	14	—	—	—	—	0
DELME THOMAS	(Wales)	14[2]	—	—	—	—	0
GORDON BROWN	(Scotland)	13	—	—	—	—	0
FERGUS SLATTERY	(Ireland)	12[2]	—	—	—	—	0
FRANK LAIDLAW	(Scotland)	10[2]	—	—	—	—	0
MIKE ROBERTS	(Wales)	10[2]	—	—	—	—	0
MICK HIPWELL	(Ireland)	5	—	—	—	—	0
STACK STEVENS	(England)	6	—	—	—	—	0
RODGER ARNEIL	(Scotland)	5	—	—	—	—	0

Key: A = appearance, T = tries, C = conversions, PG = penalty goals, DG = dropped goals.

[1] Includes one appearance as substitute.
[2] Includes two appearances as substitute.

LIONS IN NEW ZEALAND

	P	W	L	D	F	A
1888	19	13	2	4	82	33
1904	5	2	2	1	22	33
1908	17	9	7	1	184	153
1930	21	15	6	0	204	113
1950	23	17	5	1	420	162
1959	25	20	5	0	582	266
1966	25	15	8	2	300	281
1971	24	22	1	1	555	204

TESTS IN NEW ZEALAND

	P	W	L	D	F	A
1904	1	—	1	—	3	9
1908	3	—	2	1	8	64
1930	4	1	3	—	34	53
1950	4	—	3	1	20	34
1959	4	1	3	—	42	57
1966	4	—	4	—	32	79
1971	4	2	1	1	48	42

2. Lions Tour of South Africa 1974

May 15th   BEAT WESTERN TRANSVAAL   59–13
        (Potchefstroom)

W. Transvaal: Tries: Schaap, Stoffberg; con: De Bruin; pen goal: De Bruin.

Lions: Tries: David (2), Edwards (2), Brown, Steele, Moloney, Ripley, Rees; con: Bennett (7); pen goals: Bennett (3).

May 18th   BEAT SOUTH WEST AFRICA (Windhoek)   23–16

S. W. Africa: Tries: Ellis, Prinsloo; con: Karg; pen goals: Karg (2).

Lions: Tries: Edwards, Milliken, Rees; con: Irvine; pen goals: Irvine (2), Old.

May 22nd   BEAT BOLAND (Wellington)   33–6

Boland: Pen goals: Thiart (2).

Lions: Tries: Milliken (2), Grace, McBride, Edwards; con: Old (2); pen goals: Old (3).

May 25th   BEAT EASTERN PROVINCE   28–14
        (Port Elizabeth)

E. Province: Tries: Marais, Campher, Erasmus; con: Cowley.

Lions: Tries: Steele, Slattery, Davies; con: Bennett (2); pen goals: Bennett (4).

May 29th   BEAT SOUTH WESTERN DISTRICTS   97–0
        (Mossel Bay)

Lions: Tries: J. J. Williams (6), G. Evans (3), J. P. R. Williams (2), Slattery, Davies, Moloney, Old, Grace; con: Old (15); pen goal: Old.

June 1st   BEAT WESTERN PROVINCE (Cape Town)   17–8
W. Province: Tries: Read (2).
Lions: Tries: Rees, Brown; pen goals: Bennett
                      (3).

June 4th   BEAT S.A. FEDERATION XV (Goodwood)   37–6
Federation: Dropped goal: Tobias; pen goal: Tobias.
Lions: Tries: Slattery, Brown, Bergiers, J. J.
                      Williams, Milliken; con: Irvine (3); pen
                      goals: Old (2).

June 8th   BEAT SOUTH AFRICA (Newlands)   12–3
South Africa: Dropped goal: Snyman.
British Isles: Pen goals: Bennett (3); dropped goal:
                      Edwards.

June 11th   BEAT SOUTHERN UNIVERSITIES   26–4
           (Newlands)
Universities: Try: Macdonald.
Lions: Tries: Bergiers, Uttley, Brown, Kennedy;
                      con: Irvine (2); pen goals: Irvine (2).

June 15th   BEAT TRANSVAAL (Ellis Park,   23–15
           Johannesburg)
Transvaal: Dropped goals: Bosch (2); pen goals:
                      Bosch (3).
Lions: Tries: Milliken, J. P. R. Williams, Neary;
                      con: Bennett; pen goals: Bennett (3).

June 18th   BEAT RHODESIA (Salisbury)   42–6
Rhodesia: Pen goals: Robertson (2).
Lions: Tries: Grace (2), Steele, Edwards,
                      Slattery, Irvine; dropped goal: Irvine;
                      con: Irvine (3); pen goals: Irvine (3).

June 22nd   BRITISH ISLES BEAT SOUTH AFRICA   28–9
             (Loftus Versfeld, Pretoria)

South Africa: Dropped goal: Bosch; pen goals: Bosch
                  (2).

British Isles: Tries: J. J. Williams (2), Bennett, Brown,
                  Milliken; con: Bennett; pen goal: Ben-
                  nett; dropped goal: McGeechan.

June 27th   BEAT QUAGGAS (Ellis Park, Johannesburg)   20–16

Quaggas: Try: Stephenson; dropped goal: Kirsten;
             pen goals: Kirsten (3).

Lions: Tries: Brown (2), Ripley; con: Irvine;
             pen goals: Irvine (2).

June 29th   BEAT ORANGE FREE STATE   11–9
            (Bloemfontein)

Free State: Dropped goal: Snyman; pen goals: Sny-
               man (2).

Lions: Tries: J. J. Williams, Davies; pen goal:
               McKinney.

July 3rd   BEAT GRIQUALAND WEST (Kimberley)   69–16

Griqualand West: Tries: Wiesse (2); con: Wiesse; pen goals:
                    Wiesse, Van Eck.

Lions: Tries: Grace (4), Steele (2), Evans,
                    Moloney, David, Kennedy, Slattery, Rip-
                    ley; con: Irvine (8), Gibson; pen goal:
                    Irvine.

July 7th   BEAT NORTHERN TRANSVAAL   16–12
           (Loftus Versfeld, Pretoria)

N. Transvaal: Pen goals: Luther (4).
Lions: Tries: Davies, Neary; con: Irvine (2).

July 9th   BEAT LEOPARDS (East London)   56–10

Leopards: Try: Mgweba; pen goals: Mbika (2).
Lions: Tries: Grace (3), Gibson (2), Ripley,
             Morley, Edwards, David, Irvine; con:
             Irvine (5); pen goals: Irvine (2).

July 13th   BRITISH ISLES BEAT SOUTH AFRICA   26–9
            (Erasmus Stadium, Port Elizabeth)
South Africa: Pen goals: Snyman (3).
British Isles: Tries: J. J. Williams (2), Brown; dropped
                    goals: Bennett (2); con: Irvine; pen goals:
                    Irvine (2).

July 17th   BEAT BORDER (East London)   26–6
Border: Pen goals: Steenkamp (2).
Lions: Tries: Steele (2), Edwards; con: Irvine;
                pen goals: Irvine (4).

July 20th   BEAT NATAL (Durban)   34–6
Natal: Pen goals: Hannaford (2).
Lions: Tries: Irvine (2), Davies, Slattery; con:
                Bennett (3); pen goals: Bennett (4).

July 23rd   BEAT EASTERN TRANSVAAL (Springs)   33–10
E. Transvaal: Try: Fourie; pen goals: Salt (2).
Lions: Tries: Grace (2), David, Ripley, McGee-
                   chan; con: Irvine (2); pen goals: Irvine
                   (3).

July 27th   BRITISH ISLES – SOUTH AFRICA   13–13
            (Ellis Park, Johannesburg)
South Africa: Try: Cronje; pen goals: Synman (3).
British Isles: Tries: Uttley, Irvine; con: Bennett; pen
                    goal: Irvine.

PLAYER		A	T	C	PG	DG	PTS
ANDY IRVINE	(Scotland)	15¹	5	26	27	1	156
PHIL BENNETT	(Wales)	11	1	15	21	2	103
ALAN OLD	(England)	4	1	17	7	—	59
TOM GRACE	(Ireland)	11	13	—	—	—	52
J. J. WILLIAMS	(Wales)	12	12	—	—	—	48
GORDON BROWN	(Scotland)	12	8	—	—	—	32
GARETH EDWARDS	(Wales)	15¹	7	—	—	1	31
BILLY STEELE	(Scotland)	9	7	—	—	—	28
DICK MILLIKEN	(Ireland)	13	6	—	—	—	24
FERGUS SLATTERY	(Ireland)	12	6	—	—	—	24
MERVYN DAVIES	(Wales)	12	5	—	—	—	20
TOM DAVID	(Wales)	9	5	—	—	—	20
ANDY RIPLEY	(England)	9	5	—	—	—	20
GEOFF EVANS	(England)	8	4	—	—	—	16
J. P. R. WILLIAMS	(Wales)	15¹	3	—	—	—	12
JOHN MOLONEY	(Ireland)	8	3	—	—	—	12
CLIVE REES	(Wales)	6	3	—	—	—	12
MIKE GIBSON[R]	(Ireland)	7	2	1	—	—	10
ROGER UTTLEY	(England)	16¹	2	—	—	—	8
ROY BERGIERS	(Wales)	10	2	—	—	—	8
KEN KENNEDY	(Ireland)	10	2	—	—	—	8
TONY NEARY	(England)	8	2	—	—	—	8
IAN MCGEECHAN	(Scotland)	14	1	—	—	1	7
WILLIE JOHN MCBRIDE	(Ireland)	13	1	—	—	—	4
ALAN MORLEY[1]	(England)	2	1	—	—	—	4
STEWART MCKINNEY	(Ireland)	8	—	—	1	—	3
FRAN COTTON	(England)	14	—	—	—	—	—
IAN MCLAUCHLAN	(Scotland)	13	—	—	—	—	—
CHRIS RALSTON	(England)	13	—	—	—	—	—
BOBBY WINDSOR	(Wales)	12	—	—	—	—	—
SANDY CARMICHAEL	(Scotland)	10	—	—	—	—	—
MIKE BURTON	(England)	8	—	—	—	—	—

[R] Sent out as a replacement.
[1] Includes appearances as a substitute.

LIONS IN SOUTH AFRICA

	P	W	L	D	F	A
1891	19	19	0	0	224	1[1]
1896	21	19	1	1	310	45
1903	22	11	8	3	231	138
1910	24	13	8	3	290	236
1924	21	9	9	3	175	155
1938	23	17	6	0	407	272
1955	24	18	5	1	418	271
1962	24	15	5	4	351	208
1968	20	15	4	1	377	181
1974	22	21	0	1	729	207

[1] At that time a try scored one point; thus just the one try was scored against the 1891 Lions throughout that tour.

TESTS IN SOUTH AFRICA

	P	W	L	D	F	A
1891	3	3	0	0	11	0
1896	4	3	1	0	34	16
1903	3	0	1	2	10	18
1910	3	1	2	0	23	38
1924	4	0	3	1	15	43
1938	3	1	2	0	36	61
1955	4	2	2	0	49	75
1962	4	0	3	1	20	48
1968	4	0	3	1	38	61
1974	4	3	0	1	79	34
Total	36	13	17	6	315	394